The Amish

YOUNG FRIENDS

The Amish

Images of a tradition

Jan Folsom

STACKPOLE
BOOKS

Published by
STACKPOLE BOOKS
5067 Ritter Road
Mechanicsburg, PA 17055

Printed in the United States of America

10 9 8 7 6 5 4 3 2 1

First Edition

Photograph titles: page i, Isaac; p. v, Knife Pleats; p. vii, Day-
dreaming; p. 146, Last Look.

The chapter "News from *The Budget*" taken with permission from
The Budget, August 5, 1992, a newspaper published in Sugarcreek,
Ohio, by Sugarcreek Budget Publishers, Inc.

Kraybill, Donald B., *The Riddle of Amish Culture,* chapter 5, "Rites
of Redemption and Purification," p. 105. Baltimore: Johns
Hopkins University Press, 1989.

Kraybill, Donald B., *The Riddle of Amish Culture,* chapter 2, "The
Quiet Work of Amish Culture," p. 25. Baltimore: Johns Hopkins
University Press, 1989.

Unless otherwise noted, Scripture quotations are from the King
James Version of the Bible.

Library of Congress Cataloging-in-Publication Data

Folsom, Jan.
     The Amish : images of a tradition / Jan Folsom. — 1st ed.
         p.   cm.
     ISBN 0-8117-2558-8
     1. Amish—Social life and customs. 2. Amish—Pictorial
works.   I. Title.
E184.M45F65   1995
973'.08'8287—dc20   94-43064
                                               CIP

To Bettina,
for encouraging the dream,
and
to Hanne,
for helping to make it come true

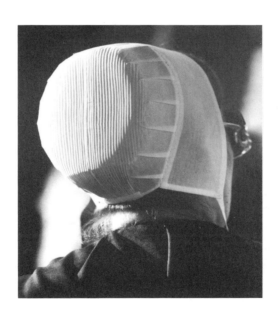

Contents

THE SWARTZENTRUBER BOY

Acknowledgments

I wish to thank all the people who have supported my endeavors to create an exhibit and book on the Amish: My friend Hanne Williams, whose unfailing encouragement, help, and belief in me have been invaluable. My aunt Grace, the most marvelous character in my life, who has shared with me her love, faith, wit, and memory of family history. Esther Smith, my high school journalism teacher, who at age ninety has been my guide, editor, encourager, and friend. My three children: Mark, for helping me take the first steps; Mitchell, for his encouragement; and Mindy, for loving care and editorial assistance. John A. Hostetler, Donald Kraybill, Stephen Scott, and Stan Kaufman for sharing their expertise on the Amish. Wilmer Otto, for believing in me and this book and for offering valuable details from his Amish family. My Amish friends in many parts of the country, especially the Atlee Millers, Monroe Masts, Alvin Masts, Mose Masts, and Joe Bowmans in Holmes County, Ohio; the Gene Mullets and Jonas Schmuckers in Indiana; and the Sam J. Hostetlers and Sam E. Yoders in Mifflin County, Pennsylvania. Bertha Schrock and Mary Miller in Illinois, and Suvilla Peachy in Belleville, Pennsylvania. Jeri Charles, who connected me with a wonderful Amish family. Tony Tucher, whose friendship and encouragement have helped me through crucial times. Sarah and Norman Glick in Belleville, Pennsylvania, and Vivian and Paul Hunt in Lancaster, Pennsylvania, for providing me with bed and breakfast, rest and relaxation, and a good measure of love. Jeannie Ferber, whose enthusiasm and experience as a publisher provided important building blocks. Carol Anderson Chandler, high school friend and editor. Nora McCray, for consistent friendship. Jay and Dorothy Kershaw, for unconditional love and support. Gretchen Huering, whose wizardry in formatting the manuscript was only part of her special care. Bob Kennedy, for his excellence in printing my photographs. Victoria Cooper, for her superb editing help. To all the Amish who have openly shared their lives with me, I am humbled and grateful for their reserved tolerance of my photography and their continued inspiration and unconditional love. I have tried to make my presentations educational and honest, without embarrassing them or betraying their confidences. And Sally Atwater, my editor at Stackpole Books, who saw in me what I didn't see in myself: that I could be a writer as well as a photographer.

WATCHERS AND WORKERS

Introduction

"Why do you come here?" inquires Atlee Miller when he squires visitors through the German Culture Museum in Holmes County, Ohio. The answer is nearly always the same: "To experience the peacefulness."

As the quality of life deteriorates in our mainstream society, there is an increasing curiosity about the Amish and their peaceful existence. Tourists leave their harried lives in the cities and flock to these rural communities to experience the beauty and tranquillity of a nearly forgotten way of life. What can we learn from the Amish? Is life as idyllic as it appears on the surface? What are their daily concerns? What is it like on the inside? Speculation and misinformation abound. My goal in writing this book is to provide fresh insights about the Amish that will cause readers to examine their own lives, reassess their own values, and gain some respect for these significant people in our midst.

Growing up in Ohio near the largest Amish community in the world, I was often taken to visit Mennonite relatives who lived in the area. Raised as a city girl and encouraged to be adventurous and creative, I felt uneasy with my shy and plain rural cousins. We lived in two different worlds, and I was unable to relate to their seemingly simplistic way of life. It wasn't until I had lived and traveled in more

than fifty countries and worked with tribal people in Asia that I realized how much I had learned to love the differences in people, and I yearned to know more about my roots.

Delving into my family history revealed that my grandparents had been "silenced" by the conservative "Wisler" Mennonite church. Unlike the Amish, who excommunicate transgressors, the Wislers would silence their offenders by not allowing them to take communion or be involved in the church community. My grandfather provoked this punishment because he wanted to be a businessman instead of a farmer. Selling his farm went against his church's belief that farming was a profession prescribed by God and engaged in by all church members. His buying a hardware store further troubled church bishops, who felt it was impossible to be in business and remain honest. The final event came when Grandpa sold his horse-drawn surrey and bought a closed sedan to carry his ten children. Their shunning seemed to affect Grandma even more than Grandpa, and she spent the rest of her life vacillating between the two worlds of plain clothes and prayer caps, worldly fashion and styled hair.

Grandpa took a dim view of the Amish, remarking, "There are devils in those beards!" Having little good to say about any legalistic system dubbed as religion, he was particularly wary of his Amish neighbors, whom he considered to be hypocrites and opportunists. Instead of seeing them as spiritual and peace loving, he saw them as wolves in sheep's clothing, a devious people hiding behind beards and pious exteriors.

He was not understanding of the Amish riddles—those areas where the Amish seem to believe one thing and practice another. They ride in cars of others while refusing to buy their own. They use telephones as long as they aren't located inside their own houses. They don't use electricity but substitute electric power with batteries and gasoline-powered air compressors. They won't put freezers in their own houses, but they'll use them in someone else's house.

Grandpa never looked at the reasons behind these inconsistencies. He didn't know that in order to keep peace among the people, occasional concessions to the rigid rules need to be made, while maintaining the overall objective to follow God's word. The more unyielding the rules, the more likely the entire system will collapse from sheer stress.

Ownership of cars is prohibited because uncontrolled use could lead people away from their commitments to church and family, into the temptations of the world. But limited use of car travel, for purposes that uplift faith, family, and community, is permitted. Telephones are banned because they could

serve as a time-wasting means for gossip. But their use out of the home is condoned by the bishop for occasional necessities. Having electric power would open the door to possession of a television set, a device for wasting time and learning worldly ways. But other forms of power would allow the use of appliances to make life easier, though not luxurious. Grandpa didn't appreciate the Amish struggle to maintain a way of life established in the seventeenth century while living in the midst of twentieth-century technology.

An outspoken Amishman in Lancaster County who yearns for change remarks, "There is no peace in the church. Peace is only on the surface. There is no open discussion between the ministers and the people, so the problems are never worked out. Our people are willingly blind!" He's dismayed at the splintering within the church because of disagreement over issues. He doesn't want to leave the church, but he wants changes to be made from within.

He believes that the leaders are arrogant dictators who levy rules and regulations without regard for what the church body wants. The leaders spell out rules against things they see as worldly for others, while allowing worldly privileges for themselves. For example, white rings on horse harnesses are considered showy, so they're forbidden, but some ministers put shutters on their houses. Rules seem to be based on tradition instead of the word of God.

Whenever we are confronted with a different set of values, we are forced to examine our own. Is there a way to adapt some of the Amish values to our own lives? Can their values touch our world and improve it?

I visited Amish families in eight states, observed their way of life, and discussed many issues with them in detail. I became as close as possible to one Amish family without actually being one of them. I met them with openness and they received me with trust. I have lived with them in their houses and they have visited me in mine. I have observed them, been with them as they wrestled with problems, and asked them questions. We have kidded each other about our differences in behavior and belief. But we have never judged each other nor expected either to change. In fact, our differences have given us a more vital relationship. What we have in common is our humanness and our love and respect for each other.

As my Amish friend Ella says, "Some people have the idea that the Amish are perfect. We're just human, like everyone else, and we have the same problems."

I understand my grandfather's feelings about the Amish. Being shunned colored his view of sects that seek to live by a multitude of rules and regulations that are difficult to follow. Living among the Amish, he saw that they often didn't live up to their lofty ideals. If he were alive, my grandfather would probably have no more understanding of my wish to spend time with the Amish than do my living Ohio relatives. In essence, their attitude is what challenged me to put together an extensive exhibit and to write this book.

During many years of travel and research in Amish communities, I have found that though the culture may on the surface appear plain and simple, in reality it is fascinating and complex. In the process of trying to disprove my grandfather, I have discovered both angels and devils in those beards.

SABBATH ON THE BACK ROAD

For Goodness' Sake

Wherefore come out from among them, and be ye separate, saith the Lord.
II CORINTHIANS 6:17

The last pin was in place. Katie's white apron and cape were secured to her black dress. Her prayer cap, starched and pleated the night before, encircled her head, ribbons tied neatly in a bow under her chin. Her black stockings, shoes, and handbag were in place. She was ready for church.

Jonas brushed the last bit of lint from his black vest and trousers and slipped into his *mutze*, a long Sunday dress coat worn only to preaching services. He fastened the hooks and eyes down the front and grabbed his black felt hat off the peg on the wall. Handkerchief and reading glasses in an inside coat pocket, he was ready for church.

It was a nice morning, and they would walk the mile and a half to Andy Miller's for church. If the weather had been bad, they would have taken the buggy. Riding in someone's car would not be permissible on Sunday as it was during the week.

To attend church in Holmes County, Ohio, members of the Old Order Amish must wear black and white clothes made to particular specifications. What would their Anabaptist ancestors have thought of this adherence to man-made rules in order to be proper in worshiping God? In the sixteenth and sev-

enteenth centuries, they gave up their lives in defiance of man-made rules in the Catholic church.

They wanted to follow the teachings of the apostles in the Bible and baptize only those who were mature enough to understand their commitment to God rather than the Catholic-prescribed infant baptism. There was nothing in the Bible that advocated baptizing babies, yet it had become a required ritual in the Catholic church.

"First you must believe, then be baptized," said those who left the church over this issue. By baptizing some adults who had already been baptized as infants, they became known as Anabaptists, meaning "rebaptizers." They were tortured and killed for their stand, and accounts of their suffering are detailed in *Mirror of the Martyrs*, an inspirational book found in most Amish homes and second only to the Bible in importance.

Clinging to Scriptures commanding Christians to separate themselves from the world, the surviving Anabaptists left the church and formed their own groups. In 1536 one group of Anabaptists followed the leadership of Menno Simons, an ex-priest from Holland. They became known as Menists and later Mennonites.

1

EARTH ART

Persecutions from the Catholic church and the government forced the Swiss Brethren to leave Bern, Switzerland. They migrated to Alsace, southern Germany, France, Holland, Prussia, and Polish Russia. In 1693 Jacob Amman, a Swiss Brethren in Alsace, proposed stricter discipline for church members and severe penalties for those who broke the rules. In addition to the existing policy of excommunication, he also advocated shunning, or social avoidance, by the community until the offender repented. He condemned trimming the beard and wearing fashionable clothing, and "anyone desiring to do so," he said, "shall be justly punished." He reinstituted the biblical ritual of foot washing and increased the taking of communion from once to twice a year as a way of nurturing faith and unity among church members. His insistence that young men adhere to the early Anabaptist position of refusing service in the military became a rule that has held to this day. Rules forbidding mustaches, outside pockets, and buttons on clothing date to this avoidance of the military and their identifying characteristics. Those who agreed with Jacob Amman's views split from the Brethren and became known as Amish.

Those who settled in Alsace were denied ownership of land. Indentured to their landlords, they endured great economic hardship. Their survival depended on families working together to make their farms productive. In spite of their struggle, the beauty of their farms was recognized throughout the province.

They were attracted to William Penn's invitation to come to Pennsylvania, where they could be separated from the world and maintain the life they believed to be godly. In the early 1700s the Amish began migrating to America, where they found freedom to practice their religion and opportunity to own their farms. Their reputation as farmers followed them to their new home, and the fastidious Swiss farms were easily distinguishable from others.

Although early Anabaptists worked at many occupations, by the turn of the twentieth century Amish and some Mennonite groups considered farming the only acceptable way to earn a livelihood. It nurtured family togetherness and promoted unity within the community. Today, developers in Amish communities, along with the growing Amish population, have depleted available land and driven up the price, forcing Amish sons to move away from home and continue the search for land that started in the sixteenth century. As a result, there are now Amish settlements in more than twenty states.

Those who migrated from Pennsylvania to Wisconsin in the 1970s, for example, found farmland for $800 to $1,000 per acre, compared to $10,000 per acre in Lancaster. Dairy farms are still available for $100,000 to $150,000 and are most often purchased with cash. Sometimes younger Amish take out loans, or families help them. Committed to a frugal way of life, they are able to live comfortably on $5,000 to $6,000 per year, and it doesn't take them long to pay off a loan.

Existing electricity on farms is left intact but not used, since electricity is forbidden. Once the farm is paid off, electric fixtures are completely removed.

Life without electricity? Without cars or telephones? Why would anyone choose to live with these and myriad other restrictions? What has encouraged

EVENING CHORES

the Amish to accept a unique set of rules that not only sets them apart from the rest of the world, but differs from that of their relatives in the next Amish district down the road?

An Old Order friend in Ohio is worried about the safety of Swartzentruber buggies on the road. "You need to be real careful of them," Ruth says, "because you're never sure what they're going to do. They're not allowed to have glass anywhere on their buggies: no windshields, rearview mirrors, windows to see through the backs of the buggies, or turn signals. The only way they can see what's behind them is to stick their heads out and look back, and that's hard to do, especially in bad weather."

Ruth's church in Ohio is a step more liberal than the Swartzentrubers. Her district allows glass, battery-operated lights, and turn signals on buggies. Their doors are made of fabric that rolls up, and the buggy wheels are metal. To have sliding doors made of wood and glass and rubber tires on the wheels, one must go up another step to the New Order Amish.

These are just a few of the unwritten, man-made rules, known as the *Ordnung*. They are unique to each district and endorsed at semiannual meetings of church members. They spell out expected behaviors, such as dress, including types of fabrics, use of buttons, head coverings, beards, and hairstyles; use of horses; and specific colors and styles of buggies.

The regulations also forbid such things as divorce, higher education, filing lawsuits, using cameras, playing musical instruments, attending theaters, owning cars, and using self–propelled farm equipment.

Ordnung rules would be impossible to accept without a vital concept known as *Gelassenheit*. Amish life is determined by *Gelassenheit*, meaning submission, yielding to a higher authority.

Unknown to modern society, *Gelassenheit* permeates the fiber of Amish life. The early Anabaptists first used it to express the idea of denying self and yielding completely to God. Through this belief, the Anabaptist martyrs went to their death without wishing revenge; instead they turned the other cheek and forgave their persecutors.

Gelassenheit determines the values, symbols, rituals, personality, and social organization of the Amish. It is a way of thinking about one's relationship to God, to family, and to others. The faithful Christian yields to God's will without trying to change things in his favor. It means suppressing selfish pursuits in order to respect and obey the decisions of the community, the rules of the *Ordnung*. It prescribes a modesty in behavior, talking, dressing, and walking. Finally, it is a way of organizing the church and social life so that groups remain small and simple. The Amish see it as obedience, humility, submission, thrift, and simplicity.

The attitude prescribed by *Gelassenheit* and the rules of *Ordnung* keep the Amish separated from the outside world and strengthen their obedience and faithfulness within the community. Their commitment to obey special rules is their way of following the biblical commandment to separate themselves from the dictates of the world, which would distract them from their relationship with God. They are committed to the belief that they need man-made laws in order to help them achieve their goal. They need to follow God's word, according to their best understanding of it, to have everlasting life.

GUIDING HAND

Gifts from God

Train up a child in the way he should go: and when he is old, he will not depart from it.
PROVERBS 22:6

They sat lined up on the sofa like little birds on a fence, listening in wide-eyed silence to our conversation. They wore identical pastel dresses and black and white prayer caps. Amy, the youngest at two, had just given up the white caps she had worn since she was three months old. Now she would wear a black one, like her three sisters, until age ten. After that, they would wear white during the week and black on Sunday until they married. Then they would wear white all the time.

Their cousins from Lancaster County, Pennsylvania, who would be arriving any moment, dressed quite differently. The younger Lancaster girls wouldn't wear prayer caps at all unless they were in church. Sometimes they wore black surplices over plain dresses of rich blues, purples, and greens. They even spoke with a little different accent. But nobody minded; it was part of the adventure of getting together.

Only the oldest of these Ohio sisters understood the strange language we were speaking. At age seven, Susan was learning English in school. Until the year before, she had understood only the Pennsylvania Dutch dialect spoken by her family.

I had not visited their home before, and the girls were fascinated at the welcome given to me, a different-looking person speaking a different-sounding language. I was surprised that these little girls were content to sit quietly for such a long time, merely observing all that was going on. I expected them to start poking each other, to become irritable or restless and vie for attention. But these little girls had learned about patience. They were used to sitting in church on a hard, backless bench for three and a half hours without diversion and without fussing. "The service trains children in the quiet discipline of waiting," writes Donald Kraybill in *The Riddle of Amish Culture*. "It is a lesson in *Gelassenheit*—waiting and yielding to time, parents, community, and God."

Large families are highly valued by the Amish, and children have the security of knowing they are wanted. The birth of a child always brings joy to a family and to the community, for children are considered gifts from God. During their first two years,

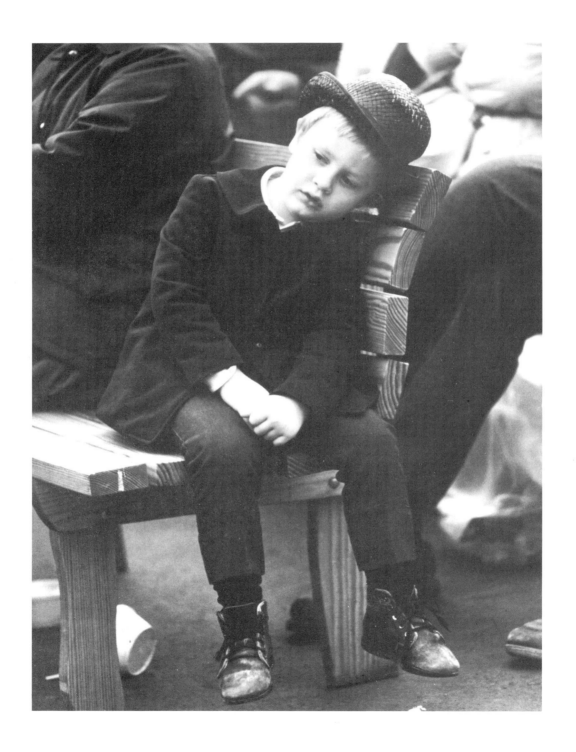

A LONG DAY

children are raised permissively with unlimited love. After they begin to walk, they start learning to be obedient. They are taught to give up their selfish will and to respect the authority of their parents. An Amish friend told me about the necessity to "break a child's spirit. It's not crushing the spirit. You just help them get it straight. You don't stifle inquisitiveness. In fact, initiative is encouraged and children are given big responsibilities at a young age." If this is not done, a child is in danger of developing hochmut, or arrogant pride, regarded by the Amish to be one of the worst faults.

Parents are responsible for the condition of their children's souls, for ensuring their eternal lives in the kingdom of heaven. Children are raised carefully within the family and community, with so much love and discipline that they feel very secure. They learn about humility, discipline, and self-control from their parents, their sisters and brothers, their cousins, and all the people who come into their lives. They learn by observing the examples around them, and the training they receive from their parents is reinforced in school and in the community, so they get a consistent message from all directions.

Now a large van pulled into the driveway. The Lancaster relatives had hired a driver to bring them to Ohio for a visit. The driver opened the van door, and a family of ten poured out. Susan and her sisters peered through the window as eight children, from six months to sixteen years, descended upon the house. Susan's older brothers greeted their cousins and helped to carry their bags. Before long, the girls were swept up in the activities and forgot their shyness.

The two families, with a total of fifteen children, had not seen each other for more than a year, and it promised to be a festive time. Every member of the host family had worked to prepare for this time with their relatives. Now they would have the great reward of playing together.

Without television as a babysitter, passive entertainment is unknown to Amish children, and they develop great skills in being self-reliant and entertaining themselves. Joe had brought his scooter and Adam had packed his Roller Blades from Lancaster. These modes of transportation were not used in Holmes County, Ohio, so it was a treat for the Ohio cousins to use them for a few days. The older boys headed for the pond behind the barn to do some fishing. If they caught anything, the fish would be added to the supper menu. The older girls went to the kitchen to help their aunt Esther with lunch. The younger ones started for the barn to see the miniature horses. After lunch these little horses, no bigger than a dog, would be hitched up to a cart, and the children would enjoy rides on the backroads through the countryside. When the corncrib wasn't too full, that was a good place to play. And every Amish family had a wagon for the children's entertainment. One of the boys liked to hitch himself to it and pretend he was a horse with a driver in the wagon. They never ran out of things to do, and much of their play consisted of creatively copying what they saw around them.

At first I had wondered why, with the measure of their discipline, Amish children didn't rebel, like children in mainstream society. But children rebel against their parents because they are unhappy, feel

DAD AND HIS TOWHEADS

neglected, or want to follow a different way shown to them by someone else. Children who are happy or have few outside influences with opposing role models have less temptation to stray from what they've been taught. As teenagers, many Amish kids learn more about the outside world and begin to test their boundaries and experiment with another way of life. But the years of immersion in a tightly knit culture and the safety net of their family and community are persuasive for more than 80 percent of them.

The result of discipline also differs according to the reason behind it. Often when a parent insists on a certain behavior for his child, it pits parent against child. But when an Amish parent insists on a certain behavior for his child, it is because he believes he has the responsibility from God to make sure his child's eternal life is ensured. It is much harder to argue with God than it is with one's parent!

In the Amish family, there is never a doubt about the importance of each member to every other member of the family. Each knows he or she is a special gift from God.

SOLITUDE

Graven Images

Thou shalt not make thee any graven image, or any likeness of any thing that is in heaven above, or that is in the earth beneath, or that is in the waters beneath the earth: Thou shalt not bow down thyself unto them, nor serve them.

DEUTERONOMY 5:8–9

Dear Katie,

I would like to come to Holmes County and take some photographs. I want to put together an exhibit on the Amish similar to the one I did on the Hmong refugees, and for the same reason: to promote understanding and acceptance among people of different lifestyles. We all have so much to learn from each other. I would like to share with others the joy I see in your lives, grounded in values much of the world has lost. What do you think?

With love to you both,
Jan

Dear Jan,

Greetings in Jesus' name. This is Sun. evening after a beautiful day. We were all in church. First trip with our new buggy. It is not fancy like Ben's, but we like it. It is black.

We just came back from having supper with Ivans. Ada's parents were also there and Ben's girlfriend, Neva.

On Thurs. we want to go and help Edna get her house ready for church.

We like your idea to spend some time here. We would like to help you with your project. There are lots of auctions in September and October, so it would be a good time to come. Just let us know when you'll be here. You know where there's bed and breakfast waiting for you. Anxious to see you again.

Love and prayers,
Katie & Jonas

And so it was that I set off for Ohio, armed with a new Nikon on each shoulder; one with black and white film and the other with color slide film. Little did I know what I was asking of my Amish friends.

In time, I learned that the Amish church in most districts opposes their members posing for photographs. The rule against glorifying an individual by displaying one's image was originally shared by all Anabaptist groups. Some eventually discarded this rule, but the Amish found Bible verses Exodus 20:4 and Deuteronomy 5:8–9 to substantiate what they believed: "Thou shalt not make thee any graven image . . . thou shalt not bow down thyself unto them nor serve them . . ." A photograph that focuses on the individual encourages a self-centeredness that is prideful and conflicts with the Amish belief in

13

humility and the importance of the community over the individual.

The day after my arrival, we set out for an auction that would benefit a man on kidney dialysis. The Amish don't carry insurance, so the community bands together to raise money for medical expenses.

"Just a word of advice, Jan," said my friends' son Ivan. "If you want a picture, don't ask. Just take it. Church rules don't allow us to pose for pictures, but if you take them without asking, no one will object. Anyway, you aren't Amish, and you won't be criticized for what people think you don't know."

Then his mother, Katie, added, "You'd better use your telephoto lens so you don't have to take a picture up close to someone." She paused. "And would you mind if we didn't sit with you?"

The guidelines set, I was a bit apprehensive, but I shot some beautiful pictures that afternoon. Comments from some of the Amish people ranged from encouraging to critical.

Since then, I have experienced various responses to my cameras. Most people don't mind if pictures are taken of their farms, houses, and horses, and they're pleased when offered a print. A father asked if I'd send him a picture I had just taken of his children. One man even took a picture of me and his children with my camera. And my friend Katie has become an expert at spotting particular shots she knows I look for.

I'm always glad when I can use my cameras to be of help to my Amish friends. Occasionally, Jonas asks me to take a picture of a scene he wants to paint on an old wood saw. A self-taught artist, he some-

times sells his painted saws in shops or at auctions. And friends who have a woodworking business are grateful for my pictures of their products, needed for a marketing brochure.

I depend on my Amish friends to give me straight answers concerning my boundaries. "If you are on the street or any other public place, you can take pictures of anything you want," Ivan told me. But even this guideline seems to vary with the area. I took a picture of a white buggy on a backroad in Mifflin County, Pennsylvania, only to have the driver become most upset with me.

"It's okay with me if you want to take pictures," head carpenter Reuben Fisher told me before a barn raising began. "But I just want to ask you to stay down by the road. It's not a good idea to get too close to all the activity where you might be in the way."

A kind man, Reuben's tactful direction was meant to ensure my safety as well as the uninterrupted progress of the carpenters. But I felt there was something else he wasn't mentioning. Barn raisings are popular events for the Amish community. They provide great entertainment for those spectators who make the effort to rise at the crack of dawn and get to them. It also provides great opportunities for photographers, and perhaps he wanted to protect his workers from trying to avoid having their pictures taken while climbing on the superstructure of a barn.

I was respectful of his wishes until I spotted a few shots that could be taken only from the yard

EIGHT-HORSE HITCH

between the house and the barn. I walked up through the lawn and discreetly snapped some good shots. Shortly afterward, I saw Reuben coming toward me. Feeling guilty that I had not obeyed him, I was surprised when he asked, "Got any good pictures?"

"Reuben, I thought you were going to scold me for being up here instead of down by the road as you asked me," I replied.

"Oh, no," he said. "That was just to keep you out of trouble around the construction area. I would be happy if you would send me a few pictures if you get some good ones."

Before the day was over, more than a dozen folks asked me to send them pictures. I was happy to oblige. I was particularly pleased to provide the owner with pictures he could display inside the barn.

Driving in Holmes County, Ohio, one spring day, I pulled off the road, up a grade, and onto a farmer's field, where I was greeted with a panorama of gentle hills overlapping and folding into each other, barren trees interspersed in the valleys in graceful silhouette. Just as I had my camera set, a team of horses appeared over the crest of the hill, pulling a harrow turning over rows of earth. Then an identical team appeared in the next furrow. My camera snapped as the two teams approached. They stopped, and I put my camera down and waited while a man from the nearer rig came toward me.

"Hey!" he yelled. "Get off my land."

I stood silently, waiting for him to plod across the furrowed field, until we were face to face.

"You're on my land. You shouldn't be taking pictures on my land," he said.

"I am sorry," I said, "I hope you'll forgive me. This is one of the most beautiful views I've ever seen. Just turn around and look—isn't it breathtaking?"

He turned around and we both stood there for several moments. Then he broke the silence. "You ought to see it in the fall. It's really something then. All those trees down in that valley are in color. You should come back and see it then . . . and bring your camera."

"Thanks," I said. "If you don't mind, I might do that. But I'm sorry for coming onto your land today."

"No feelin's," he called over his shoulder as he headed back to his horses. "No feelin's."

When I developed my film, I examined the pictures carefully, and there in the background was his friend with the other team of horses, giving me the finger!

My friends in Holmes County appreciate photos I take of their homes and gardens, but that wasn't my experience in Belleville, Pennsylvania. I stopped to take a picture of a pristine garden one day, only to see a woman come running out of the house, waving her arms and yelling, "No pictures, no pictures!" Surprised, I said, "You have such a lovely garden. I didn't think you would mind if I photographed it."

THROUGH MORNING MIST

"No pictures, no pictures," she repeated angrily. I apologized and left, wondering whether she considered a photograph of her garden as breaking the rule regarding graven images. Later, when I recounted this incident to someone who knew her, I was told that, typical of many Amish people, she had a large collection of owl figurines, graven images of a different type.

Katie gives me copies of calendars and country magazines and encourages me to send my photos and stories in for publication. When I visited Katie and Jonas recently, they asked why I wasn't taking many pictures anymore. Shooting photographs for my exhibit had taken a great deal of time and energy, and I didn't want my Amish friends to think that was the only reason for my visits. I was glad to be able to say, "I've taken the pictures I need. Now, while I'm here, I just want to be with you."

One of the great joys has been to gather around their big oak kitchen table in the evenings and, together with six or eight of my Amish friends, pass around all the slides and photographs I've taken since I last saw them. Each person who can identify people or places in a photo writes the information on the back. This is such fun for everyone that one time when I was preparing to leave Ohio again, one of the teenage boys said to me, "Jan, you can't go. What are we going to do for entertainment after you leave?"

WOMAN TALK

A Woman's Role

Favor is deceitful, and beauty is vain: but a woman that feareth the Lord, she shall be praised.
PROVERBS 31:30

She sits demurely on the plain gray, straight-backed sofa, her dress a lighter gray, blending into the background. One senses she has always sat demurely, hands folded in her lap, feet precisely together on the floor. She isn't the typical Amish woman. She hasn't had many of the typical experiences, such as caring for a husband and children or the strenuous demands of assisting with farm work. Stricken with polio as a young girl, she has endured ordeals of her own that have made her life different. Countless operations have left her legs partially functional; she is able to walk only with an exaggerated gyration of her body. The clumsy, two-inch platform sole on her left foot nearly evens her legs, but her spine is twisted.

She has been more sheltered than other Amish women, her world more closely defined by the boundaries of her property. Her most significant outings are to meetings of other Amish polio victims that take place yearly in various Amish communities. There she finds solace, companionship, and a compassionate support system.

She is a pretty woman, with fine features and flawless skin belying her forty-five years. She would have been sought after as a wife had she not been crippled. But polio rendered her unable to do the heavy labor expected of a wife. She has had to find value in her life without marriage in a society where being a wife and mother are the ultimate roles for a woman.

She has been fortunate to support herself in various jobs, working in a greenhouse and doing dressmaking in her home. But her independence is crumbling as her health deteriorates, and now she must rely on work done only from a sitting position.

Because she never had the goal of wife and mother, she has gained wisdom from a different perspective. She spoke about teenage girls and her concern that marriage was their only goal: "Their goal should be, like all of us, to live their lives so that they can get into the kingdom of God and have life hereafter. Girls who are seeking only marriage are giving too much emphasis to this worldly life."

It's a tough philosophy for teenage girls. They are trained from birth to be mothers. They aren't

MOTHER'S DAY OUT

allowed education that would prepare them for professions. Jobs with any significance are frowned upon. The most acceptable thing an Amish girl can do is to be a wife and mother. How could a girl put her acceptance into the kingdom of God before her need to find a mate? Dorothy did it. But then, she is special.

"It's a good thing I'm Amish. I'd go hog wild!" Martha said while we were shopping one day. It was the first time I realized that the Amish too are tempted to fill their lives with all sorts of material possessions.

"Well count yourself lucky," I told her. "Think of all the money you save and all the needless clutter you don't have to deal with."

"You're right. It's a lot easier not having it when you know it's just not allowed."

"It's a lot easier when none of your friends have it either."

"I suppose," she said. "Some people feel sorry for us because we don't have all the stuff they do, but I can't see that they're any better off. Having to make all those choices would wear me out!"

"See that girl we just passed?" asked my elderly friend Mary from the passenger seat in my car. I glanced in my rear-view mirror in time to see a pretty blonde Amish girl in a plain, blue dress walking beside the road. "It's a story with a real happy ending," Mary continued. "She had a baby and she wasn't married. When her baby was three months old, she ran into the baby's daddy at an auction. He thought she was mad at him, and she thought he didn't love her. When they found out they loved each other, they got married, and now they're real happy together."

"Mary," I said with amazement, "I didn't know an Amish girl would have sex before marriage."

"Well, she's not supposed to, but I guess we're all human, aren't we?" she said matter-of-factly. There was no judgment in her voice. Just acceptance of the ways things were.

The older Amish choose to look the other way while the teenagers "sow their wild oats" during the years before they become church members. I had noticed the boys often buy cars, keep bottles of liquor in their buggies, dress in black leather jackets, and generally go against the tenets of the church. But somehow, I had never imagined the girls being rebellious.

"Ruth designed the bathroom with the sink here so that it would be easy to wash the children," Martha told me as she took me through the new house being built for her son and future daughter-in-law. I was amazed that a nineteen-year-old girl would have her role as a mother so clearly in mind that she would design the bathroom around her children before she was even married. We walked through the huge kitchen and a spacious living room with an alcove on

A WOMAN'S TOUCH

one end for a sewing area. From there, a woman could sew and keep an eye on her little ones. The whole house indicated well-defined responsibilities for the woman of the house.

"What if a girl doesn't like to cook or sew?" I asked.

"Hmm, I don't know anyone who doesn't. I guess she would just have to learn."

It seems so simple. Job description clearly defined. No wondering what career you will pursue, or how you will fit in, or what your identity will be. No trauma of choices. Everything is decided for you. Complete support system. Security for a lifetime. The only choice is whether to be Amish and to accept the role of wife and mother as your total identity.

"Anna has a boyfriend," Martha told me in confidence.

"How wonderful! Is it serious?" I was delighted with the news. Anna, Martha's beautiful sixteen-year-old adopted daughter, deserved proper affirmation of herself as a lovely young woman.

"She says it is. But she's only sixteen. There's plenty of time yet before she needs to think of marriage."

"When do you think that'll be?"

"Oh, I hope she'll wait 'til she's at least eighteen," Martha said. "She needs to be a little more sure of herself, and I'd like her to help at home as long as possible. And she'll have to quit her job at the restaurant when she has a house and husband to take care of."

It wasn't likely that Anna would share many of her deepest thoughts with her mother. Plans for marriage are very private and kept secret from others, including parents, until the last minute. But Anna had grown up caring for a home and children, and she had the skills to run a home of her own. She once told me about a non-Amish acquaintance: "There's a girl at work who wants to get married, but she doesn't know anything about taking care of a house and children, and she doesn't know if she's going to like it. Anyway, she's going to have a career, so she has to wait 'til she finishes college. She's worried because she doesn't know if her boyfriend will wait for her. And then she hopes she can get a job after that. She says my life is too simple, but sometimes her life looks pretty complicated to me. I know I don't have as many choices, but I like to know what's ahead, and that feels good."

"Irene's mother is feeling awful about her daughter getting married and moving so far away," Katie told me.

Sons and daughters live at home until they marry, and I could see how painful the separation could be after those years of closeness. Then I suddenly realized we were talking about distances within Holmes County.

"How far away will Ida's new house be from her mother's?" I asked.

"Oh, more than an hour by buggy."

I was pondering the difficulty of hitching up the horse and buggy in all kinds of weather and driving

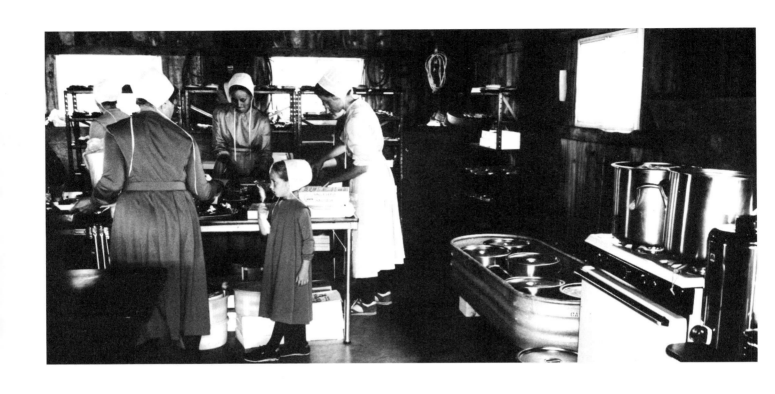

THE KITCHEN TEAM

for an hour to see my daughter, when Martha put it all into perspective for me.

"They're really going to miss her. She's such a good worker."

❧

"Susan has gone to nine weddings already this fall, and it's only October!" Ruth said.

"Susan is nineteen and pretty," I responded. "Aren't there any guys out there who want to marry her?"

"Oh yes. But she refuses to get serious about anyone until she feels she's ready."

"Is she under a lot of pressure from her friends to get married? Does she feel left out?" I asked.

"Yes, but she sees that not all her friends are happy in their marriages. They did it for lack of anything else to do. And we don't believe in divorce, so if they marry the wrong fellow, they're stuck. There are more than a few girls who wish they'd kept their feet under their father's table."

"What do they do when their marriages are in trouble?"

"Work it out," she said. "Just work it out."

❧

"Do the Amish use birth control?" I asked Edna, whose fifth child was two weeks old. I hoped my friendship with her was close enough to allow this question.

"Well, they're not supposed to," she said.

I knew better than to pursue that particular line of questioning.

"Did you have all your babies at home?"

"No," Edna said. "Everyone used to have babies at home, and some still do. But since the birthing center was built, just about everyone goes there. The rooms are really nice, and the care is just great."

"Is it staffed with doctors and nurses?" I asked.

"No, there are midwives who deliver the babies and practical nurses who take care of you and the baby."

"What if a woman has trouble during delivery? Is a midwife able to handle it or is a doctor called?"

"Sure, a doctor is called in if it is an emergency. And if they know ahead of time that there will be a problem, then you go to a hospital. But we sure like the birthing center. It feels almost like being at home, and it only costs $300 to have a baby."

❧

"Some people think our children are deprived," Rachel said, her voice rising above the clamor of happy children. "Poor kids, they don't get to see all that violence on television."

I looked about me at the sea of activity at Rachel's house. Her three sisters had convened at her house for their twice-monthly work party. Today they had made vegetable soup and fruit mush to be divided among the four families and frozen for winter use. Sixteen of their twenty-two children were in attendance—the older girls were helping their mothers in the kitchen, and the others were playing. The yard

THE GARDENERS

resembled recess at an elementary school.

Three little ones played in the sandbox. A couple of boys were hitching up two miniature horses to a wooden cart built by their grandfather. Other boys were playing with a "potato gun," which they had made out of pieces of PVC pipe and an igniter. Periodically, the lively chatter was interrupted by an ear-shattering *ka-boom* as a potato, forced down the gun barrel, went sailing into the treetops. Squeals of delight followed, then a mother's "Be careful." Upstairs, the rest of the girls dressed up in bits of adult clothing and played make-believe, a battery-operated music box playing in the background.

It was a life full of vitality and creativity and self-reliance: cooperation instead of competition, entertainment born of ingenuity, and survival dependent on everyone's willingness to work hard.

A hen party is not a social event I normally would attend. Sitting around drinking coffee and gossiping is not how I choose to spend my time. But I had just become acquainted with Mary Ellen, and she had invited me to join her and some friends at her daughter's house. And it would be a way of meeting some interesting Amish women, so I agreed to go.

Mary Ellen went ahead in the buggy, and I came later in my car, bringing the salad, following Mary Ellen's directions across the Indiana flatland.

I purposely came late, not wanting to spend too much time in idleness. But as the Pennsylvania Amish are fond of saying, "it wonders me" how I ever could have expected any Amish women to be sitting idly talking and drinking coffee. I walked into a beehive of activity.

Mary Ellen's daughter was mixing batter for three hundred cookies; another woman was setting out all the food that had been brought for lunch. In another part of the house, someone was washing the floors while the small rugs were getting a good shaking. Two others had a sewing project going in the living room, where three children were playing. There was a lot of talking; there was a lot being accomplished, too.

Working with friends is a lot more enjoyable than doing it alone. And getting together to work is better than engaging in idle gossip. Amish women have devised hen parties as a way of helping each other with projects that are too big for one person, and at the same time keeping in touch with family and friends.

Women take turns hosting these parties based on who needs help. They usually get together more frequently during the summer, when there is additional work to do: gardening, freezing, and canning fruits and vegetables for use during the winter. Even though traveling by buggy is slow and getting together is inconvenient, no one is alone. Every woman knows help is available whenever she needs it.

ON THE DUNDEE ROAD

Ben

Wherewithal shall a young man cleanse his way? by taking heed thereto according to thy word.
PSALMS 119:9

The sleek bay mare sprints through the warm afternoon air, coat glistening, mouth lathered with white foam from pulling Ben and his buggy over the hilly backroads for the last hour. Typical of horses used to pull Amish buggies, Ben's horse, Molly, is a strong, spirited standardbred, purchased off the racetrack. She wasn't fast enough to pay her keep on the race circuit, but she can pull a buggy at a steady pace forever.

At sixteen, Ben recently accumulated enough money to buy his first buggy and the horse to pull it. This is the first of only three buggies he will likely own in his lifetime. With just one seat, this one will last him until after he is married and has more children than it can accommodate. Then he will need a two-seated surrey until the children are grown. After that, a smaller buggy will take care of him and his wife for the rest of their lives.

Today he purchased an accessory for his buggy, and he is eager to get home and share it with his family, so he has allowed Molly to go faster than usual. As she slows to make the turn into the driveway, we are surprised to hear the pulsating sound of rock music emanating from the buggy.

It's a jarring sensation; the Amish seldom play musical instruments, and one becomes accustomed to the sound of silence. The only other times I've heard music in an Amish community is on Sunday mornings as hymns of praise float from the house churches. The poignant, somber ballads, written by martyred Anabaptists, are sung slowly, in unison, every note a reminder of the suffering of their Lord and their ancestors, every word cementing their identity. In comparison, the clamor we now hear is a jolting intrusion.

Ben's grandmother, Katie, and I head out the door to see the source of this ruckus.

"What in the world is that?" Katie asks, standing on tiptoe to see into the buggy. "Where's that sound coming from?"

Ben takes off his straw hat and reaches around behind the seat to a gray box attached to the back wall of the buggy.

"It's my new stereo, Grandma," he says, with some hesitation. "What do you think?"

BUGGY IGNITION

Katie adjusts her hearing aid, and with a twinkle in her eye, she says, "I think I'm really going to be glad when it comes time for you to sell it and join the church."

There is no need to lecture Ben. He is a good boy, and his temporary infatuation with a part of the outside world is normal. She knows that with patience and love from the family, this phase will pass.

I need to go to the store and pick up some items for supper, and Ben offers to take me. I boost myself up onto the step plate, then inside onto the royal blue, crushed velvet seat. A six-pack of pop sits on the floor along with a Thermos, some rope, and a black umbrella. A lap robe is tossed over the seat for cool evenings. My reflection is mirrored in the glossy black lacquer of the dashboard.

Ben turns the key in the ignition. He releases the reins, and Molly heads toward the street. I ask Ben if turning the key in the ignition starts the horse, as his grandfather says. "Is he still telling that one?" he laughs. "It's amazing how many people don't know that the key turns on the battery, which powers the turn signals and the light."

"What happens when the battery for your lights runs down?" I ask.

"We keep the batteries charged with our diesel-powered engine at home. It's the same one that runs the washing machine," he explains. "There's an Amish guy over in Lancaster who has invented a solar charger. You put it on the roof of the buggy, and it charges during the day so that it has plenty of power at night."

"Rachel's son John should have had such a device recently," I tell him. "He was out in his buggy after dark one night with a dead battery, so he had no lights. When he didn't come home, his mother and I set out in my car with an extra battery. Rachel recognized his buggy by the design of the reflective tape. When I slowed down and flashed my lights for him to stop, it frightened him and he speeded up. I turned around, passed him, and stopped, and Rachel flagged him down. There are people who harass the Amish by repeatedly passing a buggy and throwing things at it, so he had thought we wanted to cause trouble."

Ben soon turns onto a dirt side road that plunges into the woods. "Horseshoes and metal wheels tear up the roads," he tells me, "so I try to stay on dirt roads whenever I can."

He changes the tape in his new stereo to an old John Denver recording he knows I'd rather hear.

"I didn't know stereos were allowed. How will your folks feel about it?" I ask him.

"Well, I hope they won't mind too much. At least I'm not buying a car like a lot of guys. Anyway, they know it's not forever. I only plan to keep it a couple years, then sell it when I'm ready to join the church. I only hope it doesn't get stolen out of my buggy before then. Some of my friends have lost theirs that way."

"I guess you don't have any way of locking your buggy."

"Nope. It's just the chance you've got to take if you want a stereo."

It's typical for teenage Amish boys to sow some wild oats before they settle down and make their commitments to church and family. I ask Ben what they do during this time.

A VIEW FROM THE WINDOW

"I guess the most harmless thing is to decorate their buggies with lots of red and silver reflective tape. Then there are some guys who get cameras and take pictures, buy cars, get English [non-Amish] haircuts and wear English clothes, go to the movies, go to barn dances or 'keggers,' and drink liquor. They can get pretty wild. A lot of guys have a bottle stashed somewhere in their buggies." I look around Ben's buggy and wonder what he keeps in that Thermos on the floor. "Not long ago, about fifteen guys were arrested for drinking and driving, even though their horses knew the way home! It was pretty embarrassing when their parents had to go to court with them. We don't believe in suing or going to court, you know."

"How many of these fellows don't shape up by the time they are twenty-one and it's time to make the decision about joining the church?"

Ben thinks for a moment. "Not very many. I know of only one from around here. Everybody else comes around. You know, having the freedom to do these things gives us the feeling that joining the church is a choice. Then folks seem more satisfied to stay with their decision. Most guys also know that in the end, their friends and family and girlfriends are going to encourage them to stay."

I look through the fuzzy dice hanging in the front of Ben's buggy. A front window, used for protection from the winter cold, has been taken out for the summer. I enjoy the cool breeze coming through the opening, until another buggy passes us and we are covered with dust.

We start down a gentle grade, and Ben pushes on the brake pedal. There's no response. Ben pushes

again and again. Still nothing. Ben pulls back on the reins, and Molly tries to slow down, but there is no way to slow the buggy, and the shafts connected with the harness push her forward. The shortened reins twist her neck around. Ben releases the reins, and Molly breaks into a run down the hill, out of control. The buggy shudders and rattles down the rough grade. I'm frightened. So is Ben. I close my eyes, waiting for the crash. Finally the road levels out. Ben speaks calmly to Molly and pulls gently on the reins. She slows to a stop.

We sit quietly for a moment, our hearts pounding. Then Ben, still shaking, exclaims, "Why didn't the brakes work? They were fine all afternoon." He gets out to console Molly and check the brake linkage. Everything seems fine.

"There's a buggy shop just up the road. We'll stop and see if Sam can fix it."

We arrive at Miller's Coach Shop without further incident. Sam Miller's expertise is recognized not only in Amish areas of Ohio, but in other parts of the country as well. Besides Amish black buggies, he makes classy show carts for Saddlebred competition and sulkies for racing. His clients include wealthy horse breeders in addition to the local Amish.

Taking a look at Ben's wheels, Sam discovers that the brakes are out of hydraulic fluid. There's a slow leak, and they need to be replaced. We have no choice but to wait while Sam does the work.

Suddenly, Sam catches sight of the stereo. "Hey, is that a stereo you got there? How about turning it up? No harm listening to it while I work. You got any Led Zeppelin or Pink Floyd?"

SWARTZENTRUBER KITCHEN

Daily Bread

She perceiveth that her merchandise is good: her candle goeth not out by night.
PROVERBS 31:18

The great old brick oven stands in the corner of the anteroom, adjacent to the kitchen. At seven feet high and three feet square, it is large enough to serve a commercial bakery. A large iron door at the top opens to an oven with five racks. The smaller bottom door secures the fire house.

Hannah's long, dark blue skirt swirls around the edges of her hightop shoes as she enters the room. A black cotton scarf covers her head. On her gray apron is a colorful collage of the morning's productivity: flour, meringue, and raspberry jam.

As she goes about her long day's baking chores, she shows a contentment that results from achieving what she has set out to do, taking pleasure in the simplest tasks.

She leans over to put more wood into the fire. "How do you know if it's the right temperature for baking?" I ask.

"You just know," she says. "You just know."

As she opens the top door, revealing five racks of perfect pies and breads, a delicious mixture of aromas wafts into the room. Hannah slides a long wooden spatula under a loaf of bread in the back, pulling it forward to examine its doneness. Satisfied, she removes it, along with several other loaves baked in an odd assortment of pottery, Pyrex, and metal containers. She takes them on a tray into the kitchen, where a wooden cooling rack awaits.

The kitchen, with its Spartan simplicity, has been functional for nearly two hundred years. It is light and airy, with low, uncovered windows across one side. Its whitewashed plaster walls are unadorned. Yellowed pine cabinets, already antiques at the turn of the century, stand stoically, their tops gouged and scarred from serving five generations of cooks. The house was built before wooden floors were considered a luxury, and the grooved oak floors show evidence of the passage of time.

Across the window side of the long, narrow kitchen stretches a series of long tables, put together end to end to accommodate the baked goods. Hannah's daughter, Sarah, has been helping her mother since dawn, and she stands in front of a table, kneading a large tub of bread dough. She pinches off a

GIVE US THIS DAY

piece large enough to fit into an oval casserole. Other loaves sit in their containers, finishing their final rise in preparation for baking.

Sarah is fifteen. She finished school a year ago, and now she is learning at her mother's side the skills she will need for her married life.

The two women work together as a well-coordinated team, going about their work silently, not having to speak, each knowing what needs to be done and which of them will do it. Sarah prepares the bread for baking. Hannah puts it in the oven, times it, checks it, and takes it out. They work together on the pies, one making the dough, the other rolling it out, taking turns preparing different fillings and putting them in the unbaked crusts, crimping down the edges of the top crusts. They're like seasoned dancing partners. Each knows the movements so well that one steps forward when the other steps back, and rhythm sustains the momentum.

At supper time, Sarah takes over getting everything out of the oven and cleaning up so that Hannah can prepare to feed her family of six.

By day's end, they have baked fifty-three loaves of bread, forty-seven small pies, thirty-one medium pies, twenty-five large pies, two hundred moon pies, and assorted cookies. Tomorrow Hannah and Sarah will take them to the marketplace, where eager customers will be waiting to buy them.

After supper they retire to the porch, which is bathed in a soft yellow glow cast by a kerosene lamp. Muted shadows fall around Hannah and her two daughters, their homespun dresses soiled from the day's work. The painting comes to life with the rhyth-

mic rocking of Rebecca's chair, her one-year-old Thomas sleeping on her lap, his golden curls falling past his shoulders, onto his dress, tattered from the exploration of his world that day. Rebecca is living at home again, with her two children, since the death of her husband in a farming accident.

Sarah's youthful beauty radiates in spite of her long day in a hot kitchen. Wisps of hair fall out from under her black head covering. She sits with her tattered, flour-smudged dress hiked improperly to her knees. One foot is immersed in a bucket of ominous-looking liquid. Yesterday she stepped on a rusty nail, and today she stood all day making pastries for her mother. Now her foot is sore, with red streaks on her leg. She hopes the old Amish remedy of wood ashes in warm water will draw out the poison.

Hannah reaches for a bucket of freshly picked lima beans. She begins snapping the pods, scooping the beans out with her fingers into a bowl. The empty pods fall into a wooden crate on the floor.

"Hannah, how can you start more work?" I ask. "You've already done enough for one day."

Hannah's weary voice is barely audible over the cicadas in the surrounding trees. "My neighbor brought them to me. She asked me to take them to market tomorrow and sell them for her." I pull up a stool and begin snapping pods. "We're never given more work than we can handle," she continues. "When people have a lot to do, the family has to work together to get it done. The problem comes when people have too much money and they can get along without each other. Then it becomes too easy for each to go his own way."

BIDING TIME

We discuss many topics from the heart this evening, and I am pleased at the effortless way we speak, as if we have known each other a long time. And perhaps we have. We are both women who have lived a long journey, raised a family, experienced joy and tragedy, gained our own perspective on life, and arrived at some definitive conclusions. We are sisters.

The next day, I go to the shopping center where Hannah and her daughter have set up a table with their baked goods. I stop and ask Sarah, who seems to be walking quite normally, how her foot is. She responds shyly, with a pleasant, "Fine," as if there were no other way she would be.

It is noon and I am surprised to see that they have only a few items left for sale on the table.

"Hannah, it looks like your bread and pies are a great success. How much do you charge for each item?"

"Well, let's see. A dollar for the bread, three dollars for the large pies, two dollars for the medium pies, a dollar for the small pies, thirty-five cents for the moon pies, and fifty cents for six cookies."

"Hannah, those prices are too low. You hardly cover the cost of the ingredients. Haven't you ever heard of the law of supply and demand? If your goods are selling that fast, you can make fewer pieces and raise your prices and still make more money than you're making now."

"Oh," she says softly, "I couldn't do that. There might be someone who would want something and then they couldn't afford it."

TIME OUT

Rum Springa

Rejoice, O young man, in thy youth; and let thy heart cheer thee in the days of thy youth, and walk in the ways of thine heart, and in the sight of thine eyes: but know thou, that for all these things God will bring thee into judgment.

ECCLESIASTES 11:9

It's Saturday night in Arthur, Illinois. Three blocks of one-story shops lining downtown Vine Street closed hours ago. The town is deserted, except for a few folks at the IGA market buying last-minute items for Sunday dinner. All is quiet except for an occasional train crossing on the Missouri Pacific tracks at the north end of town. There's not much reason to be on Vine Street after dark, not unless you are an Amish teenager looking for more action than you can find on the family farm.

The temperature sign at the State Bank of Arthur reads eighty degrees when John pulls his horse over the railroad tracks and into a parking lot, where it joins others at the hitching post. Plastic bag in hand, John slips into a Port-O-Let and emerges looking like any clean-cut American kid: jeans, tennis shoes, and T-shirt advertising the Hard Rock Cafe. The home-made blue broadfall pants and aqua polyester shirt worn on the way in from the country will wait safely in the buggy until he returns and changes back into the typical Amish garb for the ride home.

Sauntering down Vine Street, he finds some of his buddies waiting for him on a wooden bench outside Arndt's variety store. He hangs out there with them for a while, smoking cigarettes and checking out four Amish girls sitting on a similar bench on the other side of the street. Building courage to make the first move, he is relieved to see two girls he knows riding up on bicycles, ribbons from white prayer caps streaming over their shoulders. They stop and join in the conversation.

One of the guys talks about the truck he is buying. His parents aren't pleased and won't help pay for it, but they accept it as one of the things teenage Amish boys do before they settle down and join the church. Though he's working at a lumberyard making good money, John's friend hasn't saved enough to pay cash for the truck, so his cousin will cosign a loan with him. Soon he'll have motorized transportation to haul his friends. Then they can go all the way down to Mattoon, where there is a movie theater, or to Decatur, where they can play miniature golf. For tonight, their options are limited. The only place to go in this town is the Arcade, just down the street from the Total Look Beauty Salon, across from the Disciples of Christ Christian Church, and up from the Favorite Brother Bed and Breakfast at the south end of town. At the Arcade, they can smoke cigarettes and

43

KATIE AT THE BAT

listen to rock music while they play pool and video games.

They have a friend with a television set and a VCR, so they could go next door to the Movie Palace and rent a couple of videos. Levi works there. He is twenty-one and says he used to be Amish. Levi also works part-time at an Amish tourist attraction and has no education or career plans. He feels liberated, but he has no interest in learning about computers or attaining other modern technical skills. When asked about his life goals, he says, "I just live each day at a time." His parents pray that he will come back to the fold and join the church, like his three sisters. In the meantime, they wait patiently for him to finish his *Rum Springa*, the period of running around allowed Amish youth. They have resisted making offers as Amish parents often do to motivate their children toward a decision to join the church. They can't afford to buy him a new house, and the gift of a horse and buggy would hardly be enough to sway him. They just continue to look the other way, allowing him to live at home with the love, acceptance, and values they hope will eventually influence him.

An Amish girl and boy come into the Movie Palace and rent three movies. It's ten o'clock. Will they stay up and watch them yet tonight? Or find a time and place to watch them tomorrow—The Lord's Day?

In some areas, when their parents are out of town, teenagers throw a barn dance for their friends. They indulge in liquor and unchaperoned snuggling to the accompaniment of live or taped music. In Arthur, Amish kids don't dance, so "keggers" are part of their rebellion. Sometimes they drink too much and pass out in their buggies on the way home. The horse knows the way, but it doesn't know to stay on the right side of the road or to stop at intersections. Once in a while a groggy driver gets arrested for DUI. If he's lucky, he'll get home without incident and his parents will never know what he has been doing.

Do any of the Amish kids cause much trouble?

"Yeah, they sure do," says police officer J. D. Watkins. "The older Amish never cause a bit of trouble, but some of the young ones are real devils. They get bored with nothing to do, and once in a while they start tearing up things: petty vandalism, like breaking store windows or smashing pumpkins. On occasion, we'll find them smoking pot, sometimes harder stuff. But no serious crime."

There are other causes for their mischief. Some Amish kids, like Levi, haven't even thought about what they want to do with their lives, and that puts them in limbo. Their rebellion releases them from the constraints of Amish life but doesn't give them an alternative direction. It's not like a kid whose parents want him to be a doctor, so he rebels and becomes an artist. When an Amish kid rebels, he has no alternative role models, and he has never heard talk around the dinner table that would inspire him. With just an eighth-grade education, he's not going to find a lot of doors open to him.

It's now midnight, and no adults have been on the streets of Arthur for a couple of hours. An occasional bicycle sits unguarded in someone's front yard, a monument to the trust and tranquillity in this small town. It's time for Officer Watkins to go off duty, time for the Arcade to close its doors for the night. After the stifling atmosphere in the pool hall, John finds the cool air refreshing. It will feel good going home with open windows in the buggy. It will feel good going home to sleep.

SUMMER HAT

A Tip of the Hat

. . . separate yourselves from the people of the land . . .
EZRA 10:11

A quarter of an inch? You need to go all the way to the hatmaker to have only a quarter inch taken off the brim of your hat?" I ask incredulously. Jonas shrugs, puts his hand to his bearded chin, and says thoughtfully, "That's okay. You don't have to take me. I can go with the buggy."

"No, that's not the point," I say. "I'll be happy to drive you there. I'm just surprised that such a little extra on your hat brim would make that much difference." Jonas gives me a patient smile, and without a word, he turns from the breakfast table to prepare for the morning ride.

For our excursion to the hatmaker, Jonas changes into a navy blue polyester "plain" suit made by his wife, Katie. The opening on the broadfall trousers is similar to sailor's pants, with a drop front buttoned at the waistband. Buttons, forbidden on women's clothing, are allowed on men's trousers. The jacket is truly plain, with no collar, no lapels, hooks and eyes instead of buttons, and pockets only on the inside, where they can't be considered decorative.

It's spring, transition time from winter's black felt hats to the ventilated straw hats of summer. Before going out the door, Jonas grabs his straw hat and adjusts it on his thinning gray hair. It's the first time he's worn it this season, and it feels weightless compared with the heavy felt.

As we head west for the thirty-minute trip, Jonas checks his seat belt. Our road climbs, giving us vistas of the countryside below: pristine farms punctuated with silos, cropland sculpted gracefully in the earth. Buggies pass us pulled by sleek horses, steam rising from their backs. The rhythm of their hooves echoes in our ears. Metal buggy wheels leave shiny tracks like satin ribbons, gracefully interwoven on the dirt road before us. We follow them through a verdant valley.

The signs at the end of a farm lane indicate that hats and bunnies are both available here. Our presence alerts a dog, two cats, and several chickens, which scatter behind a corncrib nearby. My car eases to a stop under a line of freshly laundered clothes, suspended from the top of the barn to a pulley at the house. The mellow browns, blues, greens, and purples

AT THE HATMAKER'S

of the dresses and broadfall trousers blur against the sky in a fluttering collage.

A small sign with HATS hand-lettered on it is tacked above a door on the barn. Once inside, my eyes gradually adjust to the dim light, and I am greeted by a myriad of new sights, sounds, and smells. The wall to my left is divided into numerous compartments, each containing a different wooden mold for a hat crown. Two walls on my right are similarly divided, holding different sizes and shapes of oak molds for hat brims. At the far end of the room, a gas lantern, the only source of light, hangs from the ceiling. In the soft glow, I see a cutting table beneath it, with scissors, calipers, and other tools of the trade. Long tubes attached to two commercial sewing machines curl off the back of the table, through a hole in the wall, to an air compressor.

In an adjoining room, the odor of wet wool hangs heavily in the air. Unshaped black wool felt hat forms, purchased in bulk in Erie, lie slouched against each other. Two steaming machines stand in readiness. John Troyer, the hatmaker, looks up from his work and greets us. He places a hat form upside down in the center of each steam machine. After pressing a wooden crown mold into each form, he stretches the brim over the brim mold and fastens clamps to hold it taut. Hot steam is forced through the felt, causing the fibers to swell and interlock into a new form. In several hours, after a hat is cooled and dry, he will remove the clamps and sew rayon lining and a leather band inside the crown and a grosgrain ribbon around the outside. The brim will be trimmed and edged with a ribbon. These custom-made hats

sell for $70 to $80. Ready-made hats, stashed in the attic of the barn, sell for about half that price.

While the two hats are steaming, John performs the simple task of cutting a bit off the brim of Jonas's hat and replacing the ribbon edging. He tells me that each group of Amish has its own type of hat. "You don't dare wear the wrong kind, or folks will think you're something you're not! Take the Swartzentrubers, for instance. They've got to wear flat, wide brims and high crowns. Old Order wear narrower brims and shorter crowns. The Beachy Amish, with their cars and electricity, don't want to be mistaken for the conservative groups, so they wear real narrow brims."

"I get it. The more conservative the group, the wider the brim and the higher the crown. Do you have any Swartzentruber hats you can show me?"

"Nope. They make their own hats. They put four-inch brims on them. Compare that with three-and-a-half-inch brims on Old Order hats. Then notice the crown. A creased crown is not as plain as a round or flat crown, and a wide ribbon is not as plain as a narrow one. Those conservative folks use real narrow black ribbon on their hats. Others use ribbon up to an inch wide. If you go over to Pennsylvania, you'll see some more interesting hats. There in Mifflin County, the Nebraska Amish have hats with even wider brims and scalloped edges. They're the most conservative group in the world. Their hats measure four-inches high in the crown, with four-and-a-half inch flat brims."

As we leave, John's young son comes in holding two bunnies. He asks if we want one. I notice that he

HAT FORMS

is wearing a black straw hat with a narrow, curved brim and a rounded crown. "See this hat?" his father points out. "These are Ohio hats. No one in Pennsylvania wears them."

Curious about fitting another piece into the hat puzzle, I drive to Pennsylvania and visit a hat-maker in Mifflin County. In Mary Peachey's workroom in her farmhouse, she braids straw, then sews the braids into spirals, making straw hats for an Old Order group, of the same name, known as the Peachey Amish. In addition to their unusual use of only one suspender, one of their identifying features is their wide, flat-brimmed hats, banded with wide,

black grosgrain ribbons. The following are the brim widths for the Peachey Amish hats:

	BRIM WIDTH
Ministers	4 inches
Other men	3 1/2 inches
Single boys	3 1/4 inches
School boys	2 3/4 inches
Little boys	2 1/2 inches

I begin to realize why an increment of a quarter inch is significant to the wearer and why a man wants to make sure his hat is precisely what it should be. His very identity depends on it.

ANNIE'S LAUNDRY

Laundry at Dawn

Let nothing be done through strife or vainglory;
but in lowliness of mind let each esteem other better than themselves.
PHILIPPIANS 2:3

I had awakened in this room many times before to the sound of a cow lowing in the distance, or to the echoing clip-clop of horses pulling buggies down the street wet from the morning dew. But this morning was different. A strange whirring sound was coming from someplace beneath my bed.

I groped for the battery-operated lamp on the bedside table, and in its dim light I shuffled to the nearest window. Pulling aside the heavy, dark blue curtains, I gazed into a white sea of fog. A dim light from the basement beneath me illuminated patterns of soft colors.

Freshly laundered clothes hung suspended from a clothesline. One end was attached to the house and the other to a pulley somewhere out in the fog. Annie knew this haze would clear with the first rays of sun, and she already had the first load of laundry out of the wringer washer and onto the line to dry. The whirring and the occasional popping that had awakened me were the sounds of the gasoline-fired air compressor running a washing machine in the basement.

Feeling the dampness through my body, I shivered, and headed for the warm bathroom. Amish-made oak cabinets stood out against practical, plastic, tile walls and vinyl floor. Everything was spotless and in order, except for a white prayer cap left lying on the counter top, along with several straight pins used to fasten a dress, worn the day before. I lighted the kerosene lantern in a holder on the wall and filled the basin with hot water. As I attempted to put on my makeup, I realized my reflection was barely visible in that lovely, dim light. I caught myself wondering how a woman could fix her hair and her face in such darkness, when I remembered that Amish women wear no makeup.

By the time I was ready to join in the day's work, Annie had the second load of laundry soaking and more water heating, and she was putting oatmeal and fresh fruit on the table. Mose was pulling off muddy boots, having just finished his early-morning farm chores. From their children's house, joined to theirs by a walkway, their grandchildren were heading out for the walk to school, black lunch pails swinging from their hands.

My day usually begins with television news, but the absence of electricity here eliminated that option.

53

THE CLOTHES DRYER

Radios, even if battery operated, are also forbidden. At first I felt uninformed not knowing the latest news. Then it was a little like being on vacation. Funny how good it felt for my mind, used to processing all that information, to be free to think about other things. Sitting down for breakfast with my friends, I listened to conversations about their concerns of the day. Nothing about the latest world disasters or man's inhumanity to man. Only decisions about how much ice to order for the refrigerator and what to donate for an auction next weekend. The proceeds would help pay for the medical expenses of a man on kidney dialysis. The Amish don't buy insurance; they take care of their own.

Our discussion of family news and plans for the day came to a close with the last bite of oatmeal. Realizing that I had slept through the most industrious part of the day, I wondered how I could contribute. "Is the laundry finished yet?" I asked.

"Oh my, no," Annie said. "I still have all the sheets and towels and clothes to do from my cousin's house. She's bedridden and can't do for herself."

I helped Annie clean up the kitchen after breakfast, then put on my warm jacket and headed out into the foggy day to string up more clotheslines.

As we hung laundry, Annie and I chatted and swapped stories, taking care to hang like items together so the laundry would not only dry well but also be visually attractive in the process. She told me about a man who was overheard remarking with some satisfaction to his wife as they left church one Sunday, "I believe you were the plainest one there today, dear."

We both laughed, knowing there was more than a little truth to the story. I always did suspect some of

the Amish of comparing their humility with others', and that, in itself, seems to be some sort of reverse humility. A sort of keeping up, or down, with the Yoders.

"We also feel that sometimes there's a kind of competition on who keeps the cleanest house. I sure don't win that one," Annie said.

"There's one you might win: the woman who gets her laundry out on the line earliest in the morning. You must be number one in Holmes County. But you couldn't compete with a woman in Pennsylvania who has an unbeatable system. She has been known to get up in the early morning while it's still dark and hang out some clean, dry clothes from her closet, so that people would think she was the first to get her laundry out on the line!"

"Oh, no," Annie said. "Now I can't believe that. Someone made that up!"

She couldn't be convinced that this was a true story, in spite of my offer of positive identification.

Annie then changed from cheerful to thoughtful as she shared a real concern. "I'm kind of worried about Sarah and John. I'm afraid they're slipping a little."

"Slipping?" I asked with alarm. "Sarah and John?"

"Well, not too bad," said Annie. "Just a little. I suppose I shouldn't worry about it."

This term is commonly used by the Amish to describe someone who is straying from church rules, and I couldn't imagine how it could apply to Annie's daughter and her husband.

Annie pulled more line through the pulley, fastened it, and picked up another handful of clothes-

NEBRASKA QUILTS

pins. "You know they just bought a bedroom set from Ivan."

"Yes, I've heard." Her son-in-law, Ivan, was a master woodworker, and he had provided every member of the family with at least one piece of his handcrafted furniture. "Sarah was so pleased to have it."

"That's the problem," Annie said quietly. "It takes some pride to have a room full of matched furniture."

To the Amish, pride is one of the greatest of sins. The church frowns upon anything that is unnecessary or impractical, anything showy that might elevate one person above another.

"Gee, Annie," I said, "you have such lovely pieces of furniture in your bedroom. That quarter-sawn oak chest of drawers that Mose made when you were first married is a treasure. I love the maple washstand that belonged to your mother, and you couldn't have nicer pieces than the walnut bedside table and the cherry cedar chest. You think they aren't fashionable because they don't match, but guess what? The 'in' thing featured in all the home-decorating magazines these days is combining pieces of furniture that are all different."

Annie caught her breath and looked at me in disbelief. "Oh, no," she said. The sudden realization that she might have inadvertently done something that was popular in mainstream society and could be considered prideful was shocking to her.

She had lived a godly life as a plain person for seventy-two years and had successfully avoided the distractions and temptations of the world. Is it possible that she had been slipping without even being aware of it?

JAKE'S REVERIE

The Haircut

Doth not even nature itself teach you, that, if a man have long hair, it is a shame unto him?
But if a woman have long hair, it is a glory to her: for her hair is given her for a covering.
I CORINTHIANS 11:14-15

Saturday night at Ivans' is always set aside to prepare for church the next day. Black jackets, trousers, and dresses are mended if needed. Crisp, sheer white organdy capes, washed earlier in the day, are given a final pressing with a gasoline-fired iron. Organdy prayer caps are taken off their forms and the tiny pleats in the back pushed together again with experienced fingers. Once every pleat is in place, the prayer caps are returned to their holders atop an old oak cabinet. There's a white cap for Martha and a black cap for her unmarried teenage daughter, Anna. Ribbons hang gracefully from the corners of the caps, twisting slightly as they crest the edge of the cabinet and fall over the drawers beneath.

It's my last evening with these good friends, and I've come to say good-bye. I slip into the room through the adjoining house of their grandparents, and no one notices my quiet entrance.

Martha sits with her newly washed and dried cape draped over her lap, smoothing out the wrinkles and straightening the edges, examining it to make sure no mending is needed before ironing it. Tomor-row it will be precisely tucked with straight pins and placed over the shoulders of her black dress, then pinned at the waist to her white organdy apron. Ivan glances up from his newspaper and grins as he catches sight of me over his half-glasses. His week's work finished, he is relaxed in a reclining chair by one of the gas floor lamps.

Shafts of light cast a warm glow on the peaceful scene, creating soft shadows. Only the hiss of the gas and the tick of a battery-operated clock on the wall break the silence.

Anna sways in the shadows as she brushes her waist-length hair. Rarely would anyone see her hair falling around her shoulders like this. Her church believes a woman should never cut her hair yet always have her head covered in an attitude of prayer. It must be parted in the middle, pinned close to her head, and covered by her prayer cap, even as she sleeps.

Ivan and Martha's two sons, Ben and Andy, sprawl across the sofa, reading by the light of a second gas lamp. At ages nineteen and twenty, they

LEVI

could find a lot of exciting ways to spend a Saturday night in mainstream America. But these options aren't available to sons of an Old Order Amish family who have chosen to live the plain and simple life.

Ben has just decided to join the church. He's sad about selling the stereo system from his buggy to a younger friend who hasn't yet made his commitment to the church. This is only one of the many sacrifices he'll make in leaving the adventurous life of a young bachelor and becoming a member of the conservative Amish church in his parents' district. Ben is always so full of fun and mischief that I wonder if he will remain in the fold or find it too confining.

He glances up at me. "Jan, do you know how to cut hair?" He hesitates. "Dad wants to give me a haircut, but I'm afraid he'll take too much off."

I look at his beautiful dark brown hair, and I wonder why it should be cut at all. It is already a trim length, ending at the curve of his head. "Sure, I'll trim it for you. It's been a while, but I think I can still do it. Get me some scissors and tell me how you want it."

He quickly appears with a beautician's scissors and a comb. He throws on a plastic cape and perches on a kitchen step stool.

Ruffling through the back of Ben's hair, I find it nicely tapered with waves falling into natural patterns. "Should I cut it the same way?"

"Yeah. Just take a little off."

From the other side of the room, Ivan intervenes. "You need to cut more than a little off!"

Not surprised at Ivan's comment, I recall contests with my own sons over hair length, and I smile while sensing a similar power struggle in this peaceful family.

"Find me a bowl I can turn upside down over his head, and I can have him looking like a Swartzentruber in no time!" I say jokingly. The Swartzentrubers, the most conservative of the half dozen divisions of Amish in Holmes County, Ohio, are notorious for their ultraconservative ways, which make them the target of many jokes within and outside the Amish community. One of the distinguishing characteristics is the men's hair—blunt-cut, straight around the head, just below the ear.

Cautiously, I snip a little off the back of Ben's neck. All eyes in the room are riveted on my scissors as another snip removes more of the controversial curve. I hate having to ignore the shape of his head, so I angle my scissors ever so slightly.

"Uh, uh, uh," calls out a voice behind me. "No tapering!"

"Oh, Andy," I say. "He's going to look like a jerk!"

"Hey, I had to have my hair blunt-cut when I joined the church. Do you think I look like a jerk?"

Until this moment, I hadn't realized the reason for this haircut: Ben was going to be baptized and join the church. From this momentous occasion on, his haircut would identify him as a church member from his particular district.

"No," I tell Andy. "Your head has a different shape. It looks okay with that kind of cut." And in truth, I admire the way his wavy auburn hair swirls into place under his father's barbering expertise. But I am frustrated that Ben's hair can't be styled so that it's

ABOUT THESE TIRES. . .

flattering to the shape of his head. Too much attention to a person's appearance is considered vain and nonconformist, and conforming is vital for the preservation of Amish culture. There is no room for individuality.

"Short enough?" I ask Ivan as Ben turns slowly on his stool.

"Nope," he says. "Cut off that curve there in the center of the back. And no tapering. It's got to be blunt-cut!"

"Ivan," I say, "where in the Bible does it say that a man has to have his hair blunt-cut to join the church?"

With laugh lines crinkling around his eyes, he answers through a wide grin, "The same place it says we have to drive buggies instead of cars!"

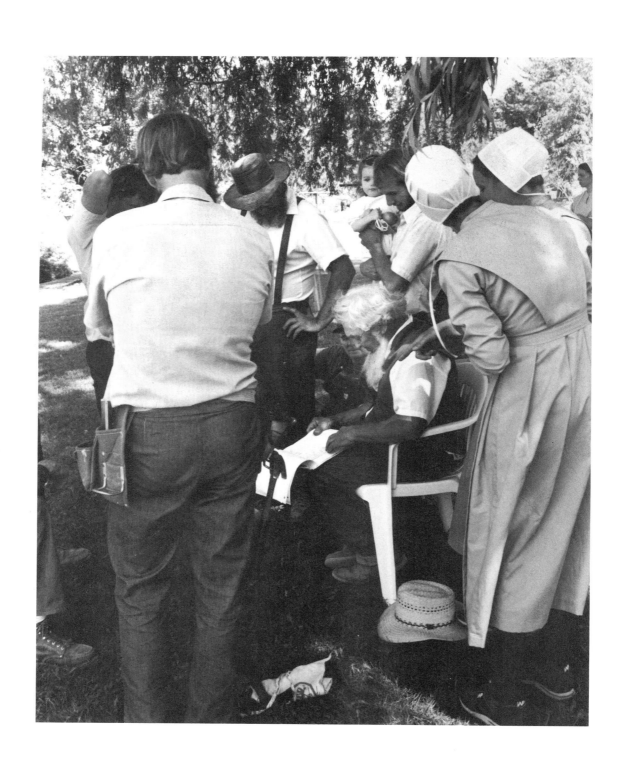

THE HEAD CARPENTER

Barn Raising

For the body is not one member, but many . . . God hath tempered the body together . . . that there should be no schism in the body; but that the members should have the same care one for another. And whether one member suffer, all the members suffer with it; or one member be honored, all the members rejoice with it.

I CORINTHIANS 12:14, 24—26.

Joe Miller never knows how many men will turn up to help with a barn raising. He just does his job as head carpenter and leaves the rest to God. It seems to work pretty well that way: More than five hundred barns are standing because of that successful combination.

It's hard to erect a barn of any size without 150 men, and on rare occasions 600 have been known to show up, leather tool belts around their waists, hammers in hand. There's a point of diminishing returns when there are more men than jobs to do, but that's a problem to be thankful for. Just the right number of men showed up on a sunny June day for Vernon Kline's barn raising. Between 350 and 400 men worked together under Joe Miller's direction, and by the end of the day, the sixty-by-ninety-foot barn was almost ready for the cows.

Vernon Kline's barn had been destroyed by fire five weeks before. It had been a substantial barn with many years of good use still expected, its life cut short by an arsonist's torch. Vernon had stored dynamite in the barn, and although it didn't explode, the

caps for the dynamite did, and the noise so frightened the horses that they ran out of the barn and were spared. But several calves weren't so fortunate, and they perished in the blaze, along with some hay and grain and the milking equipment.

The explosion woke Vernon's family, who rushed out in the middle of the night to see the fiery skeleton of their barn silhouetted against the reddened sky. Like all Amish, Vernon had registered the value of everything he owned with the treasurer of the *Brandschade*, the Amish system of aid for fire loss. Everyone in the community pays a percentage of his net worth into the fund whenever there is a fire. In this case, it was $1 for every $1,000 of worth.

First on the scene were appraisers from five Amish districts recording what was lost so that they could determine the money needed from each district. The cost of replacing the old barn was set at $45,000, not counting the calves and milking equipment. The *Brandschade* provides three quarters of the total cost, the owner one quarter, thus discouraging a man from burning his own barn. That one quarter,

65

AMISH ACROBATS

however, is often defrayed by donations of money, raw materials, and manpower: a bulldozer for clearing the debris, a truck for hauling lumber, concrete for the footers.

Within hours of the tragedy, Joe was invited to plan the construction of the new barn. During a brief meeting with the owner, he made a few sketches and they determined what kind of barn to build. A post-framed barn was planned, with mortise-and-tenon joints secured by hickory pegs. This old method of construction would produce the most solid barn possible.

Then the logistics were worked out. Joe saw that concrete was ordered for the footers and concrete block for the foundation. Vernon's son-in-law offered trees from his forest for the framing. A mill was contacted to cut the trees into framing posts and to provide boards for flooring and sheeting for the sides.

Even without telephones or cars, news of the fire spread rapidly through the Amish community. As soon as the burnt embers and twisted metal roof had cooled sufficiently, Amish and non-Amish neighbors arrived to clear the debris. After a week of cleaning up the old barn site, two dozen men skilled at setting block began the foundation. This part of the reconstruction would go quickly, but preparing the lumber for framing would be much more time-consuming. In this case, several weeks of preparation were necessary before the barn raising could take place.

Trees felled in the woods were hauled by horse and wagon to a mill, where they were sized according to Joe's specifications. Then the lumber was taken to the building site, where Joe laid the boards off,

marking each one according to its place in the framing—1 west, 2 east, for example. He made indications for mortises, tenons, and peg holes. A large notch was cut into the end of each board to be mortised. The tenon, or protruding end, of another board was cut to fit into this notch. Then a hole was drilled through the joint and a hickory peg inserted through both pieces. Some sections of the frame were pre-assembled so that on the day of the barn raising they could be pushed upright into position at one time.

As the preparations were nearing completion, the day for the barn raising, or frolic, as it is also known, was set. It was announced in the churches in every local district. Men available to work let it be known, transportation arrangements were made, details were finalized. Only inclement weather could deter the plans.

"Joe gets pretty nervous the night before a barn is raised," said Joe's friend, Atlee Miller. "There's always the concern that something might have been mismarked or that someone will get hurt. Joe never uses a blueprint. He has it all in his head. The last time, the only mistake was drilling a hole in the wrong side of one board. That was easily corrected."

The bulk of Joe's job was already done by barn-raising day. The finished foundation stood thirteen courses high, and the lumber lay in organized piles in specified areas, marked according to the order of use. The actual construction of the barn would be turned over to Joe's assistant, Monroe Miller, who would give the orders to all the men assembled.

As dawn broke, the clip-clop of horses' hooves echoed through the fog in surrounding valleys,

BEARING THE TRUSS

bringing men with their tools and women with their food to the barn site. Before the day was over, 750 would come to work and to watch.

Shortly before seven o'clock, as the first rays of sun broke through the fog, scores of men used ropes to pull and poles to push the first frame into place. This frame, consisting of upright posts attached to a crossbeam, spanned the entire width of the sixty-by-ninety-foot structure. Many of the skilled workmen dangled from beams at perilous heights while meticulously fitting the pieces together. By the snack break at half past nine, an impressive wooden skeleton was already silhouetted against the sky. The framing was completed, the braces and railing ties secured, the trusses in place and ready for sheets of metal roofing. The most important part of the structure finished, the rest of the day was spent fleshing out the skeleton into a functional barn. Only the installation of the new milking equipment remained to be done by day's end. The cows had been placed with a neighbor who had milked them during the five weeks since the barn had burned.

The men in Holmes County weren't the only ones putting superhuman effort into replacing Vernon Kline's barn. Since the fire, Amish women from six districts had organized themselves to provide food for the men building the foundation, felling the trees in the forest, hauling the trees to the mill, preparing the framing pieces for assembly, and working at the barn raising.

"Every day for five weeks, we have furnished food for lunch and snacks for the afternoon," one woman told me. "We took the food to the men wherever they were working. The church district of the barn owner determined the menu. They parceled out the food preparation to other districts. Then each of those churches had an overseer who organized it. Two women in our church shared the job. Every Sunday after church, they had a whole list of what they wanted to furnish that week, and how many dishes of each one. We just signed up, and when they had enough of that one thing, they crossed it out."

"We never knew from one day to the next how many people we would have for lunch. There have been leftovers, but we've never run out of anything."

"Barn-raising day is different. When we have weddings, we have 300, 400, 500. We know how much to fix for weddings, so we shot for 750 today. There's that many here, I think. One church brought meatloaf, another church brought Jell-O, and another brought date pudding. That's the menu today. Then there's pie and other desserts. It's a set menu. It's not like a carry-in where people would just bring what they wanted. Then there would be a lot more variation. This is all planned, so each one knows what to bring. We wanted to make sure the men had a well-balanced meal."

"A lot of women were up early this morning, preparing meatloaf and macaroni. They came by bicycle and buggy to get everything here. It's a lot of work, but it gives you a very satisfied feeling. Each one knew what to do. The girls were nominated to do certain things. My daughter is on the end there, doing dishes.

"One man rents out stoves for these occasions. Another one rents out these tables."

LUNCH BREAK

Seven kettles of noodles were bubbling as the first sitting of men approached the tables. "You can stay and eat," one woman said to me. Anyone can eat who wants to. "Everyone comes and gives of themselves."

Women served food to the men, who ate in shifts on church benches, talking over the sawing and hammering. Only after the men were back at work did the women and children sit down to eat. The children found endless opportunities for entertainment: playing in a corncrib, pulling each other in wooden wagons, playing house with the washtubs set up for their fathers to clean up for lunch. Men's hats, removed during lunch, were airing out on bushes.

Non-Amish carpenters joined in the work. "Where could you find that many of our men who would know what to do and could work together in harmony?" one man asked, of no one in particular. "No injured pride here. No four-letter words. It's a remarkable experience. It brings out the best in us. Sometimes we need to forget ourselves for the sake of a higher cause, to work together and make the world a little better."

HOUSE CHURCH

House Church

And they gathered their brethren, and sanctified themselves, and came, according to
the commandment of the king, by the words of the Lord, to cleanse the house of the Lord.
II CHRONICLES 29:15

Mom, do you think anyone would really notice if you hadn't washed all the walls?" asks Susan as she stands back to see if the calendar is rehung in the right place. She picks up a framed hand-lettered poem that has hung on the kitchen wall since she was a girl, and on her grand-mother's wall before that. It begins, "Busy, busy, too busy to pray." She finds the old nail holes, picks up fresh nails, and pounds them into place.

"I mean, have you ever thought about it, or do you just do it out of habit? It isn't like you live in the city or anything. The air is clean out here in the country. And you wash the ceilings and those walls down every time you have church just like they needed it."

Her mother, Rebecca, looks up from her ironing. "I guess others wouldn't know, but I would, and the Lord surely would. Anyway, it's just the way it's always been done."

Susan returns another item to its place on the newly cleaned wall: a rusted old tree saw. Uncle John had painted on it a credible likeness of his parents' farm, with the stream rushing through the gaping sawteeth at the bottom.

"I know, Mom. You raised me to know how to keep a house clean, but I'm beginning to wonder if we aren't overdoing it a little. When it's our turn to have church, I usually skip a few things, and it doesn't seem to make a lot of difference." She climbs a ladder and begins pounding nails above a double window, which gives her a good view of her three children playing on an elaborate wooden jungle gym built by her father. "There are five weeks yet before you're having church here, and you'll be working all that time to get everything perfect. Are you sure you have enough help for it?"

Rebecca reviews the list of available neighbors and relatives in her mind. In an Amish community, neighbors are committed to helping each other prepare for church.

"I think so. Actually, I'm going to skip cleaning out all the drawers in the bedrooms this time. I don't think they need it. When all you kids were at home I was twice as busy, but I cleaned the bedroom cup-boards and drawers every time we had church because they got messy so fast. Now some of them aren't looked into from one year to the next."

JONAS'S FARM

"I don't have that problem in our house," says Susan. "We have to move the dressers out of the bedrooms to make room for the benches for church. Do you remember when Suvilla was a baby? Her favorite thing was to dump everything out of the dresser drawers and carry half of it around the house."

"Well, she's having her comeuppance now with the twins," Rebecca says. "The Lord has His way of taking care of things. Seems like I should be going to help her, but she's coming to help me next week. She and Leanne and Irma are all coming for half a day. We should be able to get the windows washed while they're here. Then Lavina and Susanne can wash the window frames and polish the furniture when they come the week after that. I'll wash all the curtains that week, too. I'm weeding the garden some every day. Then by next week maybe it'll be warm enough to plant flowers. My sisters are coming over the last week to wash all the floors and help me with the cooking. Then all that's left is mowing the lawn. Your dad might be able to help me with that."

It is Rebecca and John's turn to have church at their house. There are thirty-four families in their church district, bounded by streams and property lines and county roads. An Amishman discontented with the rules of the church in his district doesn't have the option of joining a different church unless he moves into that district. This persuades members to accept most issues without question.

Each family takes a turn hosting the worship service at their house. Church is held every other week so that families can use the intervening Sundays for visiting with each other or friends. It would take sixty-eight weeks to rotate church duty in Rebecca's district if every family took a turn, but several young couples don't have places large enough to accommodate the two hundred who attend. It is customary in some communities to excuse newly married couples from hosting church for two years. Sometimes older people who have sold their farms and now have smaller houses are also excused. If there aren't enough large farmhouses in a district to rotate the duty for church, neighbors or relatives in the same district offer their houses. The woman whose turn it is helps get this house ready and prepares the food. In Rebecca and John's district, each eligible family has church about once a year. That is often enough to go through the extensive cleaning process.

This means sprucing up the place, inside and out. For some, it means cleaning every surface of the house, from attic to cellar. For others, it only means cleaning the areas that are sure to be seen. It's a personal choice. But a woman certainly wouldn't want to fall into the category of being a sloppy housekeeper. It isn't written in the Bible, but it certainly is in the back of every woman's mind that cleanliness is next to godliness.

It is essential to have the common areas spotless: living room, bathrooms, and kitchen. Every dish is washed, every pot and pan polished, the refrigerator and stove scrubbed. Then, if one is really fulfilling expectations, the fruit cellar would be burgeoning with fruits and vegetables, soups, and meats that had been put up in quart and half-gallon jars.

It is also the woman's responsibility to prepare food for the church—in Rebecca's case, two hundred

BETWEEN US GIRLS

people. If it is a regular church meeting, only lunch is served. If it is a longer service, such as council church, communion, or baptism, both lunch and supper might be served. In some areas, supper is forgone so that people can get home and do the chores. Where there are fewer farmers, people go home after the longer church days and collect their children, who have stayed with other families. Then the whole family returns to the church house for supper.

These meals vary in different areas. The Nebraska Amish are known as the bean soupers because that is what they serve for lunch. They also have pickles and red beets, coffee, and moon pies—pastries filled with dried apple schnitz. Serving bean soup was also a tradition with the Old Order Amish in Holmes County, Ohio, until the polio epidemic of 1952. The health department advised against serving food from common pots and platters. Now this group usually serves a simple lunch of cheese and bologna sandwiches and cookies, which can be purchased from a catering service that makes up "church orders." A typical menu for lunch in Illinois would be bread, peanut butter, apple butter or jelly, smearcase (cheese melted with milk and used as a spread on bread), pickled beets, sweet and sour pickles, seasonal vegetables, sometimes egg salad, apple schnitz, coffee, and tea, plus hot chocolate in the winter. For a long service, chicken noodle soup, cinnamon rolls, and cookies are added to the lunch menu.

Supper can be as extensive as there is time to prepare. Typical fare includes casseroles, bread dressing, sandwiches, sliced cheese, several salads, cakes, pies, and Jell-O.

In some areas, a special shed or barn is built for holding church services, but usually the house or an existing barn is used. In Lancaster County, tobacco sheds are often used. "But we found out they couldn't be used when tobacco was hanging up to dry in them," said Suvilla Peachey. "Worms would fall off the tobacco onto the people sitting below."

The men take care of cleaning the barns and mowing the weeds on the fencerows. The dairy barn is cleaned, cobwebs swept out, the walls whitewashed. Manure is taken out of the "straw shed" or "loafing shed" and fresh straw put down. Sometimes this or one of the other outbuildings is designated as the place where men put their kittel, or ivverhemm, after they arrive. This denim coat is worn over the suit to protect it while a man harnesses and hitches the horses to the buggy.

It is the responsibility of the men to take the bench wagon to the next house. This usually happens within a day or two after church, when all the benches are folded and fitted into their assigned slots, the songbooks stacked in their box. A team of field horses moves it to the new location, where it stands in waiting for the next church service.

Wilmer Otto, who grew up in an Amish family in Illinois, tells of the excitement when the bench wagon arrived at his house. "That was the signal for the beginning of a festive time. We kids crawled all over the bench wagon and played in it. Sometimes we'd make sliding boards out of the benches. The aunts and uncles would come to help with the preparations. I had to weed the garden and make sure it looked good enough. For nearly two weeks, there

SUNDAY FINERY

would be a great sense of anticipation of the church day at our house."

When the day arrives, church members enter in order: first the married men, then married women, then boys, then girls down to age seven or eight. Younger children sit with their mothers or fathers. It is traditional for men to go in with their hats on, keeping them on until the boys come in. The boys leave their hats outside and come in bare headed. Once in a while, a man comes into a service without his hat on, eliciting much speculation as to whether he has the "new belief." He likely had a spiritual experience, declaring he was "saved" and that wearing a hat to church is not biblical.

The service begins with the singing of solemn old Swiss hymns, resembling Gregorian chants, from the *Ausbund*, the Amish hymnal. They are sung without musical accompaniment, for musical instruments are forbidden. The pitch for the hymns may be given by either a man or a woman, though women are never permitted to speak in the service. The second hymn is always the *lob* song, meaning praise song, #770 in the hymnbook. During this song, the ministers go into another room, usually upstairs, and decide who will preach. If there is a visiting pastor, he is expected to preach one of the sermons.

The preachers have no special schooling. They are chosen by lot from the men in their district. First the church members vote for the man they think is best suited for the position. Then all the men receiving more than one vote are given hymnbooks. The man whose book contains a special piece of paper is designated as the new preacher. He is considered to be God's choice, not the result of a popularity contest by the members.

During the opening part of the church service, one of the pastors preaches for about a half hour. Then everyone kneels for prayer before the main part of the service begins. One of the other ministers delivers the principal message, which lasts for an hour to an hour and a half. Both sermons are in High German, difficult for the little children who have learned only their dialect at home. Then all the ministers present who didn't preach are called upon to give their testimonies. If there are no other issues, church is closed with a prayer and singing. When there is a problem with a member, a *sitz gma* (literally, an order to remain seated in church) will be called. All those who aren't baptized leave so that the issue can be discussed confidentially among the members. Before dismissal, the location of the next church meeting is announced.

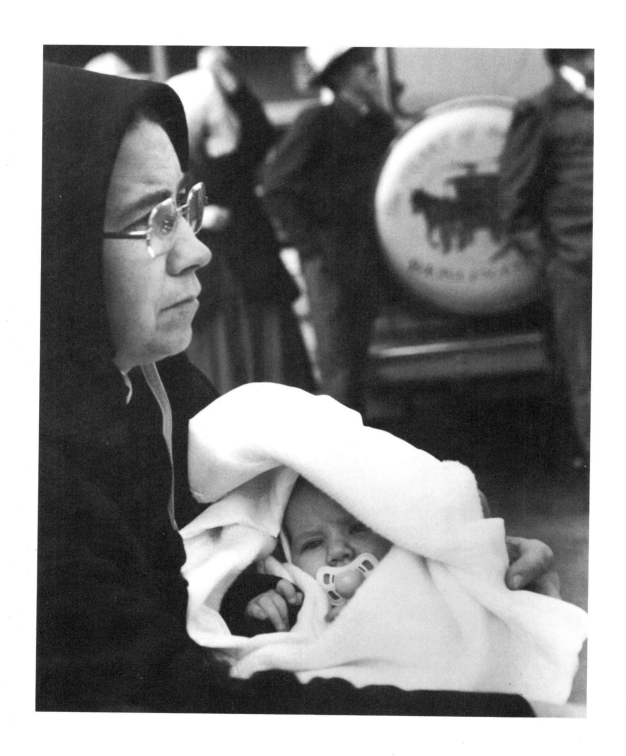

BABY IN BLACK

What's in a Name?

A good name is better than precious ointment . . .
ECCLESIASTES 7:1

Let's stop playing the Mennonite game and stop asking what your grandparents' name was and just accept people in spite of their identity," Ivan Yoder, pastor of Maple Grove Mennonite Church in Belleville, Pennsylvania, said in his sermon one Sunday. A noble thought, a new idea, but it would take more than the Reverend Yoder's admonition to his flock to change this long-established tradition.

I have heard from other non-Amish that it is hard to get to know the Amish, that they are very closed to outsiders. This has not been my experience at all, and I attribute my good fortune to my genuine interest in people of diverse lifestyles and to my ancestry. When the Plain People learn that my roots were Old Order Mennonite, that my grandparents were Mary and Jacob Horst from Dalton, Ohio, that I am truly interested in them and not just a curious outsider, doors to hearts and homes open.

The first ten minutes' conversation with a new Amish acquaintance is spent establishing identities. This is done not to satisfy idle curiosity but to fit this person into the total picture, to assess whether he or she should be respected or shunned. A newcomer is asked about his father, grandfather, and close relatives, where he lives, and what he does for a living. This process of discovery may consume the entire conversation so that nothing of any other substance is ever discussed.

In the Amish patriarchal society, one's identity is always based on the men and their lineage. But since several men may carry the same first and last names in an Amish area, names from more than one generation are necessary. Ben Raber could be Joe's Ben. In Holmes County, Ohio, there is a family who has a Sam in every other generation and a Levi in the opposing generations. No one is sure how far back it goes, but the current Sam is referred to as Sam's Levi's Sam's Levi's Sam.

Another way of distinguishing one man from another is to use a middle initial, such as Sam J. or Jake E. Professor Emeritus John A. Hostetler, an authority on the Amish, has not lived in the Kishacoquillas Valley, Pennsylvania, since his youth, but he is still referred to as John A.

81

FAMILY TREAT

To make sure there is positive identification, one can use both lineage and middle initials. Everyone in Belleville, Pennsylvania, knows who you are talking about when you refer to John Yoder as Sammy K's David R's John.

Women are always someone's daughter or someone's wife, so they are identified by the names of their fathers or husbands. Before Twyla's marriage to Merle, she was known as Sim's Roman's John's Twyla. After her marriage, she could be called Merle's Twyla or Alvin's Merle's Twyla, or Monroe's Alvin's Merle's Twyla, depending on how far back one wanted to go on her husband's side. It could be further complicated (or clarified) by using nicknames instead of given names. Twyla's mother is Benja's (short for Benjamin) Jake's Andy's May. If women were permitted to be mentioned in the line, Twyla could be added after May's name, but that isn't the way it's done.

When referring to a couple or a family, the husband's name is always used. One would never say, "Alvin and Mary are coming for dinner." Instead, "Alvins are coming for dinner." No one knows if "Alvins" is meant to be possessive or plural or both. They do know it might be just Alvin and Mary or include their whole family.

Most Amish names originated from German-speaking countries in Europe. Transferred from one culture to another, they had to go through an adjustment in pronunciation and spelling to fit into their English-speaking adopted land. Many names evolved through a convoluted series of events.

On December 16, 1742, less than ninety days after he had landed in America, Johannes Zug went to Philadelphia to apply for a land warrant. The clerk had difficulty in understanding the name as pronounced in German, with its gutteral tones and accents, and he recorded the name as Zooge. Other officials must have had similar difficulties, because the name of the original eleven Zug immigrants has been recorded as Zeug, Zuck, Tzuke, Zuke, Zuch, Zaug, Zoug, Seug, Saug, Chook, and Sook. It finally evolved into its present spelling of Zook, a well-known name in Lancaster.

A friend in Mifflin County, Pennsylvania, with the last name of Peachey traces her ancestry to a Peter Bitche who immigrated from Switzerland in 1767. In his homeland, his name was pronounced *Beechee*. In America, the spelling was changed to accommodate what English-speaking people heard: Beeche, Pitche, Pitsche, until it stabilized as Peachey. When Peter's son moved to western Pennsylvania, he changed his name from Peachey to Beachy, and this spelling has remained in Ohio for two hundred years.

Although some names ended in *e* when the Amish left Europe, that *e* was eliminated or changed to *y*; Mennonite names still end with *e*.

Every Amish community has a directory of church members and their children, including birth dates. It's updated on a regular basis, but because of the high birth rate, it's always outdated by the time it comes out in print.

My Mifflin County friend Suvilla Peachey has given me this list of the most common Amish names compiled during her visits with Amish friends. Because the Amish are frequently on the move, many of these names can be found in other areas.

LAYING A FIRM FOUNDATION

Allgyer	Lancaster County	*Frye*	Indiana
Barkman	Indiana	*Garber*	Maryland
Bawel	Lancaster County, Mifflin County	*Gerig*	Indiana
Beachey	Ohio, Indiana, Illinois, Iowa, southern states	*Girod*	Adams County, Davis County (Indiana)
Beachy	Ohio, Indiana, Illinois, Iowa, southern states	*Glick*	Lancaster County, Ohio, Indiana
		Graber	Indiana
Beechey	Ohio, Indiana, Illinois	*Harshberger*	Indiana
Bender	Mifflin County, Iowa, Indiana	*Hershberger*	Ohio, Indiana, Lancaster County
Blank	Lancaster County	*Helmuth*	Indiana, Illinois
Beiler	Lancaster County	*Hilty*	Canada, Indiana
Byler	Mifflin County, Lancaster County	*Hochstettler*	Indiana, Iowa
Bontreger	Indiana	*Hostetler*	Mifflin County
Borntreger	Indiana	*Hostettler*	Mifflin County, Indiana
Borkholder	Indiana	*Huylard*	Lancaster County
Burkholder	Indiana	*Jones*	Indiana, Kansas
Brandenberger	Indiana	*Kauffman*	Indiana, Mifflin County
Brenneman	Indiana	*Kaufman*	Ohio, Illinois
Christner	Indiana	*Keim*	everywhere
Chupp	Indiana, Illinois	*Kemp*	Davis County, Adams County (Indiana)
Coblentz	Ohio		
DeLagrange	Indiana	*King*	Lancaster County, Mifflin County
Detweiler	Mifflin County, Geauga County (Ohio)	*Knepp*	Indiana
		Kropf	Canada
Diener	Illinois, Lancaster County	*Kuhns*	Indiana, Illinois
Ebersol	Lancaster County	*Kurtz*	Mifflin County, Ohio, Indiana
Eicher	Ohio, Adams County (Indiana)	*Lambright*	Indiana
Esch	Lancaster County	*Lantz*	Lancaster County
Esh	Lancaster County	*Lapp*	Lancaster County, Hartville, Ohio
Espanshade	Indiana	*Lehman*	Indiana
Fisher	Lancaster County	*Lenecher*	Indiana
Flaud	Lancaster County	*Lengacher*	Indiana
Fry	Indiana	*Lonecker*	Indiana

RAISING THE FRAME

Mast	everywhere	Speicher	Mifflin County
Maust	Indiana	Steury	Indiana
Miller	everywhere	Stoll	Canada
Mullet	Indiana, Illinois	Stoltsfoos	Lancaster County
Nisley	Alabama, Georgia	Stoltzfus	Lancaster County
Nissley	Alabama, Georgia	Strickler	Canada
Nolt	Indiana	Stutzman	everywhere
Otto	Illinois	Swarey	Mifflin County, Center County
Peachey	Mifflin County, Lancaster County	Swartz	Indiana, western states
Peight	Mifflin County (Indian descent)	Troyer	everywhere
Petersheim	Lancaster County, Ohio	Wagler	Canada, Indiana
Plank	Illinois, western states	Weaver	Ohio, Indiana
Raber	Ohio, Indiana, other states	Weingard	Indiana
Renno	Mifflin County, Lancaster County	Wenger	Mifflin County
Riehl	Lancaster County	Wickey	Indiana, other states
Ropp	Iowa	Witmer	Indiana
Sceury	Indiana	Wittmer	Indiana
Schlabach	Indiana	Yoder	everywhere
Schmidt	Canada, Indiana	Yutzy	Ohio, Indiana, Kansas
Schmucker	Indiana	Zehr	Indiana
Schmuker	Indiana	Zook	Lancaster County, Indiana
Schrock	Indiana, Illinois		
Schwartz	Indiana		
Shapler	Ohio, Indiana, other states		
Shrock	southern states		
Slabach	Indiana		
Smoker	Lancaster County		
Smucker	Lancaster County		

In some places, names are incredibly common, prompting a popular joke among the Ohio Amish:

Q. What happens when you take all the Yoders out of Holmes County?

A. It's deyoderized.

THE GRAPEVINE

That Wonderful Home Cooking

*But meat commendeth us not to God: for neither, if we eat,
are we the better; neither, if we eat not, are we the worse.*

I CORINTHIANS 8:8

We'll expect you for lunch tomorrow about noon," were Ruth's parting words to me. I had nearly refused to join her and Paul for the midday meal because I was afraid they would make too much of it and disrupt their workday. But I agreed on the condition that it be kept very simple.

When I came up the front steps the next day, the fragrances of that wonderful home cooking greeted me. "Ruth, you made a big meal. You weren't supposed to do that."

"Oh, it's nothing special," she said. "I had to cook for Paul and me anyway."

I surveyed the sumptuous display on the kitchen table. We sat down, bowed our heads, and prayed silently. Then the best fried chicken in the world slid onto my plate, followed by mashed potatoes and gravy, fresh corn, pickled beets, pickled eggs, applesauce, coleslaw, homemade bread, fresh butter, tomato jelly, and a Jell-O salad.

I savored each delicious flavor, one after another, and my vote for the tastiest dish went to the mashed potatoes. "Ruth, these are the best mashed potatoes I've ever tasted. How did you make them?" I asked innocently.

"Oh, they're nothing special," came her reply. "Just mash 'em up with a half cup of butter and a half cup of cream cheese."

"Have another piece of chicken. How about some more potatoes? Here, you didn't get very much of this."

Then, "Better finish that up. There's not enough left to save. We wouldn't want it to go to waste!"

"I made a special dessert for you today," Ruth said, setting before me an enticing, colorful concoction called fruit pizza. This is one of Ruth's specialties, and she claims it is simple to make. First, bake a crust of flour, butter, sugar, baking powder, and nuts. On it, spread a mixture of cream cheese, whipped

TILLERS OF THE EARTH

cream, and powdered sugar. Then, top with sliced fruit artfully arranged to disguise the calories. Cover it all with a clear, sweet, fruity glaze, and you have the best dessert in Holmes County.

That wonderful Amish cooking might taste good, but it's not necessarily good for the Amish. Farmers working hard in their fields consumed that tasty, high-cholesterol home cooking for three hundred years without effect, but as farming gives way to more sedentary occupations for the Amish, there is now some awareness that diet must change in order to maintain health in a less active body. There is a little effort to use less lard and butter in favor of vegetable oil and lower-fat recipes.

Surprising to those who think the Amish exist solely on their traditional cooking, pizza is one of their most popular foods. And they must set a record for the highest consumption of carbonated drinks per person.

Still, the traditional foods are an important part of the Amish identity, and they continue to be served at weddings, funerals, auctions, reunions, family get-togethers, and barn raisings.

BARN RAISING DINNER MENU

These festive social gatherings feature food prepared in a cooperative effort by the wives of all the workers. Here is a typical menu for 175 men:

115 lemon pies	16 loaves bread
500 fat cakes	pickled beets and eggs
(doughnuts)	cucumber pickle

15 large cakes	6 pounds dried stewed
3 gallons applesauce	prunes
3 gallons rice pudding	1 large crock stewed
3 gallons bread pudding	raisins
16 chickens	5 gallons stone jar white
3 hams	potatoes
50 pounds roast beef	5 gallons sweet potatoes
300 light rolls	

The main ingredients of these recipes, total:

867 eggs

330 pounds flour

120 pounds sugar

25 pounds cornstarch

19 pounds butter and lard

22 quarts milk

7 cups salt

HAYSTACK

A Benefit Haystack was held in Arthur, Illinois, to raise money for an Amishman who had had open-heart surgery. About 150 families from five districts planned this dinner, prepared it, served it, and cleaned up after it. The $7,000 raised from donations that day was submitted to the hospital, which was so impressed with the prompt payment in cash that they reduced the bill and wiped the slate clean. The remainder of the money will go for future medication and treatment.

Build a "haystack" by heaping on your plate,

OUTDOOR MARKET

in order: rice, hamburger sauce, lettuce, tomatoes, cheese, eggs, Doritos or Ritz crackers, onions, peppers, olives, peanuts, and hot cheese sauce. Serves about five families.

> 28-ounce box Minute rice, cooked
> 8 pounds hamburger. Brown with chili sauce and chili seasoning to desired flavor and consistency.
> 3 heads lettuce, chopped
> 8 tomatoes, chopped
> 20 hard-boiled eggs, chopped
> 3 to 4 pounds cheddar cheese, grated
> 1 1/2 pounds Doritos, crushed
> 1 box Ritz crackers, crushed
> Cheese sauce: 6 cans Campbell's cheddar cheese soup heated with 6 cans milk
> Chopped onion, bell peppers, olives, and peanuts

Because of my Mennonite background, I am familiar with one favorite Amish dish: pickled eggs. The highlight of our family reunions was always the huge crock of pickled eggs brought by my grandmother. It's easy to pickle eggs, but my grandmother used to say, "You've got to make it sweet enough and sour enough, or it'll taste like dishwater."

MARY'S PICKLED BEETS AND EGGS

12 eggs	3/4 cup brown sugar
2 pounds beets	1 stick cinnamon
1 cup water	4 cloves
1 cup vinegar	

Hard-boil eggs. Cook beets until tender, slip skins off, and slice. In a large pan, heat water, vinegar, and brown sugar and spices. Add sliced beets. Add peeled eggs and cover. Wait at least twenty-four hours before eating, until the eggs have turned deep red.

Pork and sauerkraut is a popular Pennsylvania Dutch dish that originated in Germany, where it is still found on most menus. There, however, it is sour, not sweet sour. When the Amish and Mennonites crossed the Atlantic, they must have developed a sweet tooth, because they began adding sugar to everything, even meats. Pork and sauerkraut is a Pennsylvania Dutch tradition served at midnight on New Year's Eve.

RUTH'S PORK AND SAUREKRAUT

6 pounds pork loin	2 pounds sauerkraut
flour	1/2 cup brown sugar
salt and pepper	1 cup water
1 teaspoon ginger	

In roasting pan, dust pork with flour and brown on fat side. Season with salt, pepper, and ginger while browning. Add sauerkraut, brown sugar, and water. Cover and bake for three hours at 325 degrees. Serve with mashed potatoes.

The 1936 *Pennsylvania Dutch Cook Book* contains Amish recipes that are still used. Before the days of

THE CANTALOUPE WAGON

cholesterol consciousness, we thought this was the best piecrust in the world.

TWO DOUBLE-CRUST PIES

3 cups flour	1/2 teaspoon salt
1 cup lard	ice water

In a large mixing bowl put flour, lard, and salt. Lightly cut through with a pastry cutter or a knife and fork until lard is pea-sized. Add ice water while lightly fluffing mixture with a fork. Roll out on a floured surface.

Often served for breakfast or for Sunday night supper, scrapple seemed to be a popular dish with everyone in my family except me. When I was a little girl, I used to disgust my friends by reading them this recipe out of the same cookbook. The Amish make scrapple whenever hogs are slaughtered.

SCRAPPLE

Separate one hog's head into halves. Take out the eyes and brains. Scrape and thoroughly clean the head. Put into a large kettle and cover with 4 or 5 quarts of cold water. Simmer gently for 2 to 3 hours, or until the meat falls from the bones. Skim off grease carefully from the surface; remove meat, chop fine, and return to the liquor. Season with salt and pepper to taste and 1 teaspoon of powdered sage. Sift in granulated yellow corn meal, stirring constantly, until the mixture is thickened to the consistency of soft mush. Cook slowly for 1 hour, watching carefully, because it scorches easily. When sufficiently cooked, pour into greased oblong tins and store in a cool place until ready to use. Cut thin slices and fry in hot fat until crisp and brown.

ANDY

Andy

Andy was only eight years old when he began fashioning wooden toys from scraps of lumber in his father's cabinet shop. Like other Amish kids, he didn't have electronic games or sophisticated toys. His entertainment depended on his ingenuity and creativity with available resources. He would come home from school and play at his father's side, using saws and drills and sandpaper and glue to create wooden puzzles and animal shapes. Sometimes they had movable parts. Other times he would attach wheels. Andy had a special talent. His parents, however, did not encourage him to develop his talent so that he would excel above others. That is not the Amish way. That would conflict with their belief in suppressing the individual and supporting the community. They encouraged him to make toys because it was a wise use of his time, and his toys could be given to friends and relatives and to customers of the cabinet shop.

After seeing the enthusiastic response to the toys, Andy's father decided to close down his cabinet shop and manufacture small wooden products full-time. They would be interesting to make and easy to market. It would, however, take many more small items to produce the same income as he had earned with his cabinets, so Ivan set up an assembly line with additional workers. Andy and his mother, Martha, his brother, Ben, and his sister, Anna, all learned how to operate the gasoline-powered tools. Before long, they were able to handle all the areas of production.

By the time he was finished with school at age fourteen, Andy had a full-time job with his father. While the rest of the family made wooden household items, Andy designed and made toys, which sold faster than they could be produced. His special gift, however, was designing and making inlaid model trucks. He worked long hours every day except Sunday, and as his skills improved, his modest income also grew.

Andy could have become successful on his own and made a name for himself, but the importance of the family and his church-nurtured attitude of humility overrode any desire for individual attention.

THE WOOD SHOP

Although his toys were in great demand, he sold them for modest amounts of money and spent most of his time working with the family on other products.

He never went through the rebellious stage most teenagers go through when they're trying to be adults and need to test their boundaries. Amish kids are allowed to experiment with life before they join the church. Andy's defiance of the rules amounted to installing a stereo system in his buggy and decorating the buggy with jazzy reflective tape.

One time when I was leaving to go back to Ohio, Andy looked at me wistfully and commented, "You'll probably be on a plane in a few hours, won't you, Jan?"

"Yeah, and I'm going to miss all of you," I replied.

"I sure would like to go with you," came the unexpected response.

It was then I noticed a touch of sadness in the eyes of this teenage boy. I caught his realization, for just an instant, that his yearning to be adventurous, to know how it feels to soar through the air, would never be fulfilled. Because flying was against his church's rules, this was one experience he would never have.

"Andy, " I said. "I would take you with me if I could. You know you are welcome to visit me in Colorado any time you can come and any way you can get there. But I admire your discipline, and I encourage you to be who you are. You have a way of life the rest of us can learn from."

By the time I paid my next visit to Ivan's, Andy was ready to reject the English world. "Come on, Andy, tell me the truth," I said. "Don't you have a secret desire to move away from the country into the city where the action is?"

"Good heavens, no!" came the response. "Getting into all that traffic and pollution when we go up there to the bank is enough for me. There's nothing I need there. It's all right here."

Like 85 percent of his peers, Andy is content with being Amish in Holmes County, Ohio. Their choice to remain in the fold contributes to the population growth of the Amish, which doubles every twenty years. That's not to say Andy doesn't have frustrations with being Amish. When he was nearly twenty years old, his family invited me to stay for supper. I noticed him fidgeting with some stubble that seemed to be growing unevenly on his chin. He caught me looking at him. A little embarrassed, he explained: "I'm trying to grow a beard and it's driving me crazy. It itches all the time."

"Why don't you shave it off?" I asked. "You're not getting married, are you?"

It is customary for Amish men to let their beards grow when they marry. But first they must join the church, and I knew Andy had not been baptized and had not yet taken his vows.

"Oh, no," he replied. "I'm joining the church in a few months, and in our district, guys grow beards when they join the church."

It wasn't long before Andy was sporting a fine beard, outlining just the edge of his chin. In time, it would become a long, untrimmed beard, but like all Amish men, Andy wore no mustache.

A year later, I arrived in Ohio to visit my friends and discovered a new stable and a newly framed house on the family property.

WAITING FOR MARTHA

Aha! I said to myself. This can mean only one thing.

I found Andy and his father working on the house, and I asked him directly, "Andy, are you getting married?"

They looked at each other, with giveaway grins, and Ivan replied for Andy, "Jan, you have to promise to keep this secret. It hasn't even been announced in church yet, and nobody's supposed to know. But it'll be announced in two weeks, so I guess it's okay. But don't tell anyone."

"I'm getting married on October second," Andy spoke up.

"How can it be a secret when there's a new house, sitting there on the family property for everyone to see?" I asked.

"Well, everyone can have their suspicions, but no one talks about it until it's been approved by the church and it's official. That usually happens about a month before the wedding. This is traditional. It's a private matter between a couple. A lot of times, parents don't even know until it's ready to be announced at church."

"Okay," I said, "I won't breathe a word of it to a soul. Now, do I get a tour of your new house?"

I had been in many Amish homes, but I still was not prepared for what I saw. A new, forty-five-hundred-square-foot house with central heating, five bedrooms, and three bathrooms is not what I would have expected for a young Amish couple just starting out. It had been carefully laid out and seemed practical in every way. The large kitchen would be able to accommodate a big table where at least twelve friends and family members could gather together and eat. But there would be no recessed lighting, granite countertops, tile floors, or plush carpeting. Vinyl would cover every floor in the house. There was no dining room, no fancy entrance, no crystal chandeliers—just hooks in the ceilings to accommodate gasoline lanterns.

There was a living room that would be lived in, with a sewing area at one end. Instead of a television room, there was a finished basement for overflow children and guests, with an auxiliary kitchen for summer canning. The bedrooms were small and simple, and every room had practical, wood-paneled wainscoting. Skylights, once thought of as luxuries, were a practical substitute for electric lights. Family members with woodworking skills had contributed a beautiful, handmade, rolltop desk, an oak sewing machine cabinet, beds, and other pieces that would last more than a lifetime.

On Andy's wedding day, he owed $5,000 on his house, and he'd have that paid off in a few years. Then he would have only the expenses of property taxes, upkeep, and gasoline for heat. Water came from a natural spring.

Andy would never spend his money on college tuition or living away from home, on motorcycles, cars, maintenance, insurance, gasoline, clothes, CDs, videos, or pets. He will do without some of the things he would like to have experienced in life, but he has found a lot of joy in a close, fun-loving family and in a predictable life. "If you are willing to work hard and put your values in the right places," Andy said to me, "you can have it all."

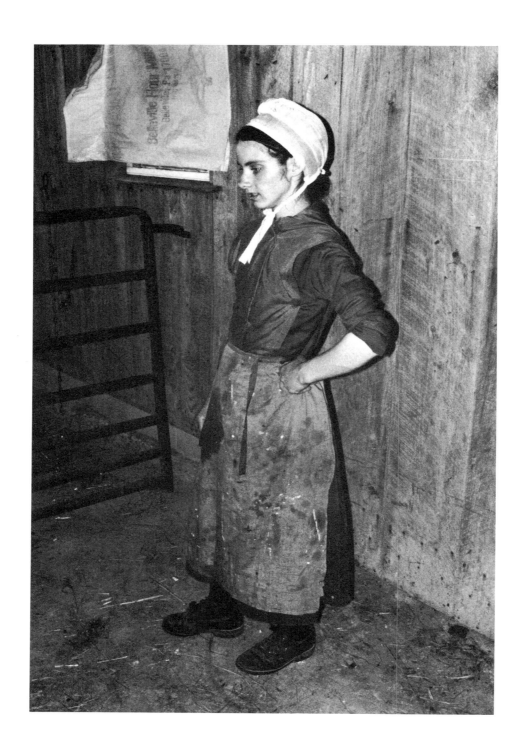

MIRIAM

Amanda

She riseth also while it is yet night, and giveth meat to her household, and a portion to her maidens. . . .
PROVERBS 31:15

The long, narrow lane cut a straight swath through the cornfield. Grooves made by the metal wagon wheels were deep enough in places that the center mound scraped the undercarriage of my car. Dust swirled behind the car, obscuring the scene in my rear-view mirror.

At the end of the lane sat a shabby old frame farmhouse. Its front porch sagged and the columns supporting the weathered roof leaned this way and that. A hundred feet from the house sat an unpainted barn.

The first time I came to Amanda's house, streaks of dark, muddy colors disappeared behind trees and outbuildings as I drove up. Eight children, unused to a motor vehicle coming down their lane, had fled into hiding. Curiosity gradually overcame fear and suspicion, and grimy faces framed with straw hats and black prayer caps poked around corners to peer at the stranger and her dusty car. Feeling like an extraterrestrial, I approached cautiously, knowing my every step was being watched.

A pretty woman in a homespun cotton dress the color of wood smoke and a stained black apron appeared, a baby in her arms. The children gathered around as I introduced myself, waiting to see whether I was friend or foe. They were barefoot and dirty, their clothes tattered and smudged with food and dirt, the boys' bobbed hair, unruly and matted, sticking out from under their hats.

Amanda had decided to sell her quilts. Normally, Swartzentruber quilts are made for personal use, not for commercial purposes, so I felt privileged to have the opportunity to own one. Amanda needed the money to buy a good wood-burning stove. The one she had was old and small and had no reservoir for heating water. A new one would cost $1,800.

Amanda welcomed me and opened the rusted, splintered screen door. I entered a kitchen very different from the spotless ones of my Old Order Amish friends. This was a primitive kitchen of a poor Swartzentruber family, not unlike cooking areas in tribal villages halfway around the world. An old

103

STONE HOUSE ON THE BACK ROAD

porcelain sink was attached to the wall, but it had no water spigot. A pump fed by a natural spring stood between house and barn; it supplied unlimited amounts of water to those willing to carry it.

Two unmatched pine china cabinets stood on either side of the wood-burning stove, and at the end of the room were benches and a long table covered with brown oilcloth. Bottles of freshly canned peaches and plums and the remnants of the canning process covered every flat surface. Flies were gathered at pools of syrup.

The gray walls were soiled from many little fingers, and faded black curtains hung at windows with torn screens. Noticing my glance at the windows, Amanda said, "I need time to dye those curtains again. They're supposed to be black and they keep fading."

"Are black curtains determined by your church?" I asked.

"Yes," she nodded, "and gray walls. And the wood trim should be painted dark gray, but we just haven't had time to do it. We've only had this farm three years, and it's all we can do to keep it running."

Amanda led me past the living room's sparse furnishings into a bedroom, crowded with two beds, where she and her husband and two children slept. Her quilts were exquisitely made in a simple patchwork of somber colors, unlike the colorful, carefully designed quilts made for sale by other Amish groups. In all, I came away from Amanda's house with five quilts that I consider treasures, even though my other Amish friends say they are "duller than dirt." Having taken the family's only means for warmth, I collected

five blankets for them, and some of my Amish friends offered this family their extra wood-burning stove.

When I returned to Amanda's to deliver the blankets and the offer, the children did not try to hide but came up to my car to greet me. Seeing their mother's gratitude, they brought armfuls of vegetables from their garden and placed these, along with several jars of Amanda's canned peaches and pickles, in my car.

Several months later, I visited Amanda again. This time the distance didn't seem so far, nor the lane so long, and the children had become my friends. The baby, by now about seven months old, was sitting in a hickory rocking chair in the living room, a diaper tied around his middle and around the back of the chair so that he wouldn't fall over. Amanda asked me whether I thought the baby seemed healthy. She was concerned because she had already lost one child to an unknown disease, and another was mentally slow. The genetic abnormalities within the Amish communities because of intermarriage during the last three centuries have given Amish mothers an extra cross to bear. Some problems are unique with the Amish and have led to the establishment of a children's hospital in Lancaster, where these abnormalities are researched and treated.

"I think he seems a bit lethargic and his skin is blue," I told her. "Compare his face with Emma's." I led the little girl to stand beside her brother in the rocker. "Have you taken him to a doctor?"

"Well, an Amish doctor came to see him."

"An Amish doctor?" I knew the Amish did not believe in schooling beyond eighth grade, so I was

FRONT PORCH

confused about what an Amish doctor could be. "What did he do?" I asked.

"He looked in the baby's eyes and said he probably had a problem with his lungs or his heart. Then he gave us some herbs for him. But I don't see any difference."

"Amanda, would you consider taking him to a Mennonite doctor?" I didn't know her beliefs about medical treatment.

"Yes, I've thought of that, but that means taking him to town in the buggy, and I don't have anyone to watch the rest of the children."

I offered to help, but she told me she'd have to talk it over with her husband.

I left that day wondering whether the baby would get help or whether he would be a victim of the system that existed in that family, in that ultraconservative church, in that community.

I didn't see Amanda and her family again for eight months, and I was apprehensive as I drove down their lane.

As I approached the house, I saw smoke curling into the air above the roof, proof that the new stove was working fine. But best of all, the baby was now red cheeked and alert, the smallest member of the dirt-covered mob that ran out to greet me when they saw my car, yelling, "Colorado! Colorado! Colorado's here!"

THE SCHOOL ROOM

Instruction in Wisdom

The fear of the Lord is the instruction of wisdom; and before honor is humility.

PROVERBS 15:33

We're not opposed to education, we're just against education higher than our heads." This opinion, offered by one Amishman, sums up the reasons Amish schooling is limited to eight grades.

"Among all the Amish people in Lancaster County," says another, "you couldn't find one who ever took any high school, college, or vocational school education. Yet I don't believe there's a class of people in the entire world that lead a happier life than do our people on the average."

Feeling that an elementary education is enough for agricultural workers in a close-knit community, the Amish have fashioned schools that they believe provide their children with all they need to lead fulfilled lives. Those who spend too much time in school are said to have "chairmindedness," a condition of many professional students in America. They are considered to be takers and not givers: They absorb information but fail to make a real contribution to the world.

In the early 1900s, the Amish attended small, local public schools. When schools were consolidated, enlarged, and removed from rural communities, the Amish struggled to have their own schools. After winning the battle against the governments in many states, the Amish began building their own schools in 1950 reinstating the values they seek for their children.

Schools are close enough to home that children can walk rather than be bused. In the intimacy of the one-room school, children are taught to work together in a supportive group, just as they will in the adult Amish community. An eight-month school year has been established so that children can help with spring planting. Parents select the teachers, who instill Amish values instead of "worldly wisdom"; parents also choose the curriculum and books. In these schools, the children find reinforcement among their own kind instead of corruption from worldly friends and an education that would lead them away from farm and faith and undermine the church.

HIDE AND SEEK

Esther spoke with a lilting Pennsylvania Dutch accent, her prayer cap framing her face. Holding a baby in her arms, she told me what it had been like when she was a teacher. She would still be teaching in this little one-room school if she hadn't married. In Amish schools, male teachers can be single or married, but when a girl marries, her home becomes her full-time job.

Esther gave me this philosophy of Amish schooling:

> Enter to learn the good you can,
> Leave to serve your fellow man.

"We teach by example," she said. "Respect is so ingrained that titles aren't necessary, so the children call their teachers by their first names. We don't grade on the curve or encourage competition. That would elevate one child above another. Instead, the children are taught to help each other. Then everyone feels better when anyone improves."

"How do you handle a child's special talents?" I asked.

"Since a person's individual talents are a gift from God, no one should be praised if he is a fast learner, nor should he be criticized if he is a slow learner. There is a place for each person God has created. Such differences are respected by the teacher and the children. Learning is directed toward conforming with what we believe is right, not toward discovering new knowledge. We don't stress curiosity, we stress acceptance."

I asked her to tell me about some of the other differences between public schools and Amish schools.

Esther shifted her baby to her left arm and went to the blackboard to make two lists.

AMISH SCHOOLS	PUBLIC SCHOOLS
Run on a human scale	Run as an organization
Cooperation and humility	Competition and pride in achievement
Group identity	Individual achievement
100 percent parental support	Partial parental involvement

"In some states, Amish children go to school only until they are fourteen years old. Here it is sixteen, but kids can stop going to school at fourteen and do home projects for another two years. We believe that a girl's training at home with her mother and a boy's training on the farm or at a job with his father both prepare them for life. We don't condone higher education for our own people, because we feel it can lead to arrogance, pride, and a haughty spirit. But we don't have a problem using non-Amish doctors. We also don't use home schooling as a substitute for regular school, because it deprives children of learning experiences found only in a group."

"It must be difficult handling eight grades at one time," I said. "What subjects are taught?"

"Reading, writing, and arithmetic are taught, and a lot more, too. Children learn to speak our Pennsylvania Dutch dialect at home as their first language. They don't learn to read and write it until they start school, and then they must learn the old German

RECESS

script. Religion, English, geography, and science are also included, but of course, they don't learn anything about computers. We didn't used to teach history, but now books are written by the Amish, offering Anabaptist history combined with American history.

"A teacher does not require any extra education. Teachers are chosen from those who did well in school and who really enjoy children. Fathers of some of the children make up the school board, and they make all the decisions. Anyone over eighteen is eligible to be hired as a teacher, but 85 percent turn out to be women. The board works with the parents in deciding how much they can pay a teacher, and they collect the money from all the families. Teachers are paid by the day. If they aren't there one day, the substitute gets it. It's usually $25 to $30 per day. Men get paid a little more because they have families to support.

"I know people think the Amish schools are pretty outdated. But a lot of learning takes place here, because there is such a peaceful atmosphere of cooperation and support. Our kids are testing in the top 10 percent of American schoolchildren. But more than that, no child feels alone or unsupported. I'm happy that my own children will go to this school."

Some of the Amish in more liberal groups seek special training. They need additional education in order to work in hospitals and other service jobs.

"Don't think the learning process ends when we're out of that one-room school," says Ruby Yoder. "Most times that's just the beginning." Ruby left her

Amish family and community in Ohio and became part of the Amish group in Sarasota, Florida. There, she passed her GED test, then took further training in health care and in teaching English as a second language. Since then, she has gone to Mexico and Romania with mission organizations to teach English.

"Do you really believe this?" asked Wilma Yoder, an Amish woman in Nappanee, Indiana, after she had finished reading the above material.

Taken aback, I replied, "Yes, I wouldn't have written it if I hadn't thought it was true."

"There is another side to this issue that you should mention," Wilma continued. "Teachers can't teach more than they know themselves. Some teachers are better than others, but at best, their knowledge is limited to what they learned in eight grades of parochial school. After the sixth grade, our daughter had learned everything her teacher knew, so the last two years in Amish school would have been a waste of time. We took her out of parochial school, and put her into public school, and she finished the last two grades there. She liked the competition. It stimulated her motivation and she was a very good student."

Wilma picked up a scrapbook and showed me news clippings and photographs of her daughter being given high achievement awards in academics and sports.

"It's a good idea for our children to start out in Amish school. It's a continuation of the values they learn at home, and they learn to read German. They

A STEP IN TIME

need to know that for church. When our daughter was old enough, we felt she needed to have someone teach her who had at least a twelfth-grade education. She was going to go to public school until she was sixteen, but she didn't like some of the things they were teaching. A class in body health turned out to be focused on rehabilitation after being on drugs."

This view was not shared by another Amish woman in a different part of Indiana who started her children out in public schools so they would have the opportunity to play with various kinds of children. After a few years they switched to a parochial school in order to become steeped in Amish tradition and be less likely to be tempted by the worldly life. About 50 percent of Amish children in Indiana go to public schools. It is one of the few states where Amish families have the choice.

But the opinion of Ruth Ann Schwartz Burkholder, a retired Amish school teacher from Bern, Indiana, is representative of the majority. She likes Amish schools because children can be taught morals that are lacking in public schools. She believes that honor rolls and other awards go against the beliefs of the church. "We don't seek honor or promote pride in accomplishment. In my way of thinking, the parochial schools are sufficient," says Ruth.

BOY MEETS GIRL

Bed Courtship

Prove all things; hold fast that which is good. Abstain from all appearance of evil.
I THESSALONIANS 5:21-22

The party was over. Her friends had left, some in their cars, some in their buggies. Her sisters and brother were fast asleep, and her parents had just retired to their room. The day had been one to remember, but for Fannie it wasn't finished yet.

She pulled the clips from her hair and removed her prayer cap. Then she took a small mirror out of a drawer, and in the flickering light of the kerosene lamp she studied her face. She didn't look any different. Still the same green eyes and dark lashes. Still the same fair complexion that flushed when she was embarrassed or stayed too long in the sun. But she felt different inside. Today she had reached a milestone. Today she had turned sixteen. This coming of age would entitle her to some long-awaited privileges. Now she would be old enough to join the youth group and attend Sunday evening singings. Now she would be free to go out and socialize with other young people on weekends. Now she would be eligible for courting.

She held the mirror with one hand, and with the other she began removing the hairpins that had held her hair in place at the back of her head. As her long, dark hair cascaded over her shoulders, she wondered how it would look if she cut it—just a little, just around her face. Many of the other girls in her area of Ohio were doing that nowadays. It was their bit of rebellion during their *Rum Springa* years. It was tricky trying to tuck bangs and short wisps of hair up under their caps, but it was worth it to enjoy this different look for a brief time. Soon enough they would join the church and never be allowed to cut their hair again.

But tonight she had more urgent matters to think of. Opening a dresser drawer, she carefully removed a fluffy mound of pink ruffles. Holding them up to herself, the ruffles fell free to the bottom edge of a fancy dress. It had three pretty buttons on the bodice—buttons that she would never be able to wear once she was a church member. And its little fluttering sleeves would allow her arms to be bared. Tonight she would wear it for the first time. It was her *nacht ruck*, or night dress, made especially for bundling, a method of courting used by the Amish since their beginnings.

AT THE FLEA MARKET

Fannie laid out the dress on her bed and ran her hand over it, smoothing out the wrinkles. Smiling to herself, she recalled all the effort that had gone into creating this dress. If her parents had only known how much time Fannie had spent thinking about the design of it, they would have considered it self-indulgent and a waste of time. Only her cousin Susan knew.

Susan lived in Indiana, where the night dresses were made in an entirely different style, and she had offered to give Fannie an Indiana pattern for her dress. At first, Fannie had felt compelled to conform to the acceptable local style. Then she decided to break tradition and dare to be different by making a dress unlike the plain night dresses her friends wore with their boyfriends. And she especially loved this shade of pink.

Fannie took off her dark blue shoes and navy stockings and slipped out of her plain gray dress with the matching apron. Once these were put away, she carried the lamp into the bathroom. Quietly, so as not to disturb her sleeping family, she washed up and slipped into her new night dress. She felt refreshed and expectant as she listened for the hum of Josh's truck.

Like other teenage Amish boys, Josh was taking advantage of his freedom to experiment with the non-Amish world. He looked like any other clean-cut American kid with blue jeans, sneakers, and a nicely styled haircut. He had bought a four-year-old Chevy truck with money he had earned working in his uncle's cabinet shop. He knew these pleasures were only temporary: By age twenty or twenty-one, Josh would be baptized and take his church vows, committing to give up the worldly life forever.

He had driven his truck to Fannie's birthday party in the afternoon, but according to tradition, he had left with the others and would return only after dark for his date alone with Fannie. Unmarried couples usually do not keep company during the daytime, when others might see them together. Often, relationships are kept secret.

Kerosene light still in hand, Fannie stood admiring her bedroom. Her mother had helped her move her belongings from the bedroom she had shared with two younger sisters to a large room recently vacated by her newly married sister. Now she had room enough for her bed and dresser, a small sofa and chair, an old table, and a little braided rug her grandmother had made for her from old clothes. Not all families could afford to give so much space to a teenage daughter. She was grateful to have such a perfect place to entertain her friends.

Placing the lamp on the bedside table, she speculated about the night ahead, the first of many she would spend with a date. She was excited but apprehensive. There was a little knot in her stomach. She liked Josh well enough, but they had never been alone before. The only times they had been together were at community gatherings: auctions to raise funds for Haiti Relief and for a school in Mount Eaton, the festival at Sugarcreek, her cousin John's wedding, the barn raising in Farmerstown. Josh had never held her hand or kissed her. This would be their first night of getting to know each other.

She had never heard her parents speak about bed courtship. Most of the Amish she knew just accepted it because this was the way it had always

UNDERDRESSES

been done. Hundreds of years ago people in small primitive houses with no heat had doubled up with their overnight guests. Bundling was a way of being hospitable to travelers and to prospective mates. Even after houses were built larger with adequate heating, the custom continued. It was such a fixed Amish tradition that a preacher who dared to speak out against it fifty years ago was silenced for five years.

Each group has its own way of practicing courtship. The Nebraska Amish girls in Mifflin County, Pennsylvania, wear two dresses during the day. At night, they remove the dark, homespun outer dress, revealing an underdress of lighter-weight fabric that is lavender, hot pink, or another bright color. Pieces from worn-out underdresses occasionally show up in otherwise somber quilts.

Some Amish groups have opposed bed courtship as contrary to biblical teachings because it puts temptation in the path of their young people. Even if practiced with decorum, it conflicts with the Scripture from Thessalonians commanding Christians to "abstain from all appearance of evil." Bed courtship was one of the principal reasons the New Order Amish split from the Old Order. New Order's rules prohibit young people from dating until age eighteen or until after they are church members. Then the girl can entertain a boy in the living room of her parents' house, not in her bedroom. The boy must leave by midnight, and there is no dating on Saturday night, which is reserved for preparation for church. If there's nothing spiritual about courting, they believe the relationship won't hold.

Teenage groups opposing liquor and bed courtship have emerged in several Amish communi-ties. In Ohio, the In-between Group arranges volley-ball and baseball games, youth meetings, and ice cream socials as substitutes for bed courtship.

But in Fannie's district, bed courtship was still regarded as the acceptable way to get to know some-one. No one ever spelled out the rules, but it was understood that sex would not be part of it. Fannie was well aware of this rule, but she had also over-heard her girlfriends talking among themselves about how exciting it could be. And she was aware that occasionally girls became pregnant. The penalties for pregnancy could be severe. Couples who became pregnant and were not church members could join the church and marry fairly quickly if they wished. But those who were already church members were banned for four to six weeks, then reinstated if they made a confession and an apology to the members of their church. After a period of repentance, they were permitted to marry.

Fannie was jogged out of her thoughts by the murmur of Josh's truck pulling into the driveway by the barn. She had asked him to park away from the house so that the engine noise wouldn't awaken her parents. She wondered if he'd remember her direc-tions for entering the house and finding her bed-room.

Footsteps ascended the creaking stairs. A flash-light flickered, and he was standing at her bedroom door holding a large radio, his jacket open, his visored cap at a jaunty angle. Her anticipation turned to apprehension. Perhaps she had fantasized about this moment too long, had built it up into unreal expectations. Suddenly, Josh didn't seem quite as handsome or as tall as she had thought. Maybe she

YOUNG MAN FROM TROYER CHURCH

shouldn't have agreed that he come tonight. Maybe she should have waited until she knew him better.

Fannie smiled shyly and walked toward him, self-conscious, hoping he felt more comfortable than she did. The expression on his face changed from confidence to wonder as he continued to stand there wearing his hat and jacket, holding his radio and his flashlight, not coming in and not going out, frozen in place and looking at her as if he had never really seen her before. It seemed like a long time before he started to speak, telling her how beautiful she was.

His unexpected outpouring surprised them both, and she felt both pleased and embarrassed. Too shy to look at him, she lowered her eyes, as her mind searched for words. After a few awkward moments of silence, she motioned for him to come in and closed the door behind him. He put his battery-operated radio on the table with the lamp and tuned it to a country music station, turning the volume low.

Following her lead, he sat down on the little sofa, taking care not to sit too close, not to brush his trousers against her bare leg. Fannie thanked him for coming. He said it was a nice party, her birthday party. She thanked him for the card and the present he gave her, a book about wildflowers. He said he was glad he hadn't drunk much liquor at her party, or he would be sleepy by now, and he sure wanted to stay awake for his date with her. He thought again how pretty she was. He thought about kissing her, then thought better of it. Finally, he found the courage to reach over to take her hand. Just as he was about to touch her, he glanced down and realized he had never taken off his jacket or his cap. His hand, destined for

Fannie's, stopped in midair. Laughing at himself, he bounded to his feet, grabbed the cap, and skipped it across the floor to the door. He took off his jacket and tossed it in the same direction. That lightened the mood, and they began to giggle. He sat down on the sofa again, this time much closer to Fannie, and she felt no inclination to edge away. He leaned over, untied his shoes, and casually kicked them off. Now more at ease, he settled back into the sofa, his arm pressing against Fannie's. He reached over and gently took her hand, so small and white next to his, rough and callused from hauling lumber and constructing wooden cabinets.

He wouldn't allow himself to say anything more to her from his heart, afraid of seeming too eager. So he talked about the volleyball game at Fannie's party and the way the ball kept going out of bounds and rolling down the hill. Fannie liked talking with Josh. He had different ways of looking at things, and she found that interesting. And she liked holding his hand. She wondered if he would kiss her. She hoped he would, but she didn't want him to know what she was thinking. Eventually Josh put his arm around her and drew her close. Impulsively, he found her mouth and kissed her. Fannie didn't resist.

Was it too soon to suggest that they go to bed? he wondered. He didn't want to rush her, but he knew she was aware of this age-old ritual and had prepared for it, as he had. He took a deep breath, withdrew his arm, and spoke softly. At his whispered suggestion, Fannie nodded shyly and walked over to the bed. Embarrassed, she avoided his glance and began turning down the covers.

GIRLS' GAME

"My grandmother made this quilt for me," she said, breaking the awkward silence. "She made it for my sixteenth birthday. Most grandmothers give quilts to their granddaughters when they get married, but Grandma wanted to give this to me now. It's called 'Grandmother's Flower Garden.' You see, she chose my favorite colors, pink and lavender." Her fingers trailed tenderly over the meticulous appliquéd seams outlining the flower petals. "Look, Josh, the stitches are so tiny and hidden, you can't see them without a magnifying glass."

Josh came to Fannie's side and leaned over, straining his eyes in the dim light. "What a lot of work!" he exclaimed. This was the first time Josh had actually examined a quilt. Sometimes when he came home from school, a group of women would be gathered around a quilt stretched on the big wooden frame his father had built. They made a real hen party out of it, sewing and eating and telling stories and laughing, all the time keeping track of the amount of thread being used so that they would know how to price the quilt if it was sold. But he had always thought of a quilt as a utility item, a cover to keep him warm while he slept. Now, because Fannie had opened his eyes, he began to appreciate the love that women expressed through this intricate needlework.

Suddenly aware of the attention that had been given to this room, to this night, Josh determined to make the time special by giving Fannie all the attention and respect she deserved. He would take off his shirt, he decided, but leave his jeans on. After all, this was just his first date with Fannie. His hands found the buttons on his shirt—buttons that would not be

permitted once he joined the church—and he opened them one by one.

Watching Josh out of the corner of her eye, Fannie wondered how much he would take off. She knew from her girlfriends that guys sometimes leave their trousers on. But sometimes they don't.

Josh struggled with one button that had become tangled in loose threads from the buttonhole. Finally, he hung his shirt on a chair back, turned off the radio, and put the flashlight on the bedside table. Fannie bent over the kerosene lamp and blew it out. They both slipped under the quilt, and after a few awkward moments, Fannie nervously asked him about his favorite things to do. Josh told her he enjoyed fishing and making things out of wood—not ordinary things, but pieces that would show off the beautiful grain. Then he started to tell her about his truck and the new seat covers he was getting, but he thought better of it, stopped in midsentence, put his arm around her, and drew her closer.

As they caressed, they talked about the next day, when he would be in church and she would be visiting her cousins. They lived in different church districts with preaching services held on alternating Sundays. Generally, boys visited their girlfriends only on the Saturday nights they didn't have church. But in some areas, after spending the night, a boy might go to church with his girlfriend's family and attend the singing with her on Sunday night. It was no surprise for an Amish family to see their teenage daughter's boyfriend come down the stairs and appear at the breakfast table on a Sunday morning.

Eventually, after much whispered conversation,

LEVI AND LIZZIE

Josh and Fannie drifted off to sleep. When they awoke, it was four o'clock, and the first streaks of dawn were just creeping across the sky. Eager to leave while it was still dark, Josh dressed quickly and picked up his radio, flashlight, hat, jacket, and shoes on his way out of the room. Fannie tiptoed down the steps after him, and after another brief kiss, waved good-bye.

She could hardly get back to sleep for thinking about her night with Josh. She couldn't have wished for a better first date. Josh had acted in a very commendable way. She thought about things she wished she would have done differently, like showing more interest in his family. But she felt generally contented; it had been a successful and memorable milestone in her life.

At six-thirty, her sister poked her head in the door and called Fannie to help with breakfast. Fannie resisted responding to her sister's inquiring smile. What had happened on her first date was her secret, and she wasn't ready to share it with anyone, especially her little sister.

Reluctant to take off her pink dress, she kept it on while she made her bed, humming as she tucked the quilt around the pillows. Her reverie was interrupted by her mother's call. She quickly took off her pink dress, folded it, and put it back in the drawer. Without wasting a moment, she put on her navy blue stockings and a plain blue dress with a matching apron, pulled her hair into the familiar bob at the back of her head, and quickly covered it with a prayer cap. "Coming," she called down to her mother. "I'm coming to help with breakfast."

ELLA'S CHILDREN

Rachel

Her children arise up, and call her blessed; her husband also, and he praiseth her.
PROVERBS 31:28

Like a leading lady on center stage, she sits with regal bearing on an old wooden chair in the middle of a huge kitchen. A spotlight of late afternoon sun shines on her through the window, washing the room in amber and gold. Her husband, David, and six of her nine children sprawl around her on the floor and on long benches by the great oak table.

As they engage in the delicious business of devouring quantities of ice cream and root beer in lieu of supper, Rachel's contentment in mothering this brood radiates throughout the room. She has happily discarded the idea of cooking another meal today: The large meal she provided for her family during the middle of the day will have to do. She treasures these special moments when the importance of family time overrides the demands of her daily routine—a routine that may include making trousers for her husband, baking pies for her family or a barn raising, hoeing weeds, canning vegetable soup for the winter, doing the twice-weekly laundry with a gas-powered wringer washer, hanging the clothes to dry, pressing them with a gasoline-fired iron, and hitch-ing the horse to the buggy for grocery shopping.

Curled up in her lap now are Danny, a toddler with platinum hair, round blue eyes, and smudges of fresh strawberry ice cream on his face, and Leanne, whose dark curly hair and brown eyes set her apart from the rest of the family. Without being asked, the older girls have begun collecting dirty dishes, clean-ing the kitchen, and wiping sticky faces.

Four children at Rachel's feet, barefoot and wearing the day's activities on their clothes, beg her to relate adventures from her childhood. As she begins, all squirming stops. Faces upturned, eyes focused on their mother, the children listen with rapt attention to the familiar stories. Rachel suddenly stops in mid-sentence. Thomas, the impetuous five-year-old, is the first to jump in. He finishes her sentence and continues with an outrageous plot of his own devising. Everyone squeals with laughter, and the game is under way. Now Thomas must continue the story until he stops in mid-sentence and someone else takes over as storyteller. These inventive stories can string on for hours, often entertaining the family for a whole evening.

NANCY'S HOUSE

Rachel thrives on the challenge of raising nine children. She would have ten, but one daughter died after a long battle with a difficult disease. Another child is handicapped and requires special care. But the Amish follow the biblical commandment to love one another, and they regard her as a special blessing, giving them an even greater opportunity to love.

Rachel struggles with her oldest son, a teenager in his rebellious years. He wears a black leather jacket, blue jeans, and a baseball cap. Although he earns decent money in a lumberyard, he drives a car and hangs out with kids who drink and carouse. He is insolent and disrespectful toward his parents.

He walks into the living room and flops down on the sofa without speaking. Rachel continues to treat him with love and acceptance. She knows this phase will pass.

She is troubled by her husband's decision to leave farming and work for a company making wooden pallets.

Like other Amishmen, David has found he can't make enough money for his large family on farming alone. Now, the money he brings in is adequate, but his boys are being denied a way of life Amish boys have enjoyed for three hundred years: growing up beside their fathers, able to see them as role models and teachers.

Traditionally among the Amish, the roles of girls and boys have been clearly defined: Girls are taught how to be wives and mothers by their mothers, and boys are taught farming skills and carpentry by their fathers. But all that is changing. Amishmen in every community are leaving their farms. In Indiana, for instance, 80 percent of Amishmen are no longer farming.

The absentee father syndrome is taking its toll. Family roles are becoming blurred. As in mainstream America, Amish women must figure out what to do with their boys after school and during the summers. The boys no longer have a predictable future. And the women are burdened with even more responsibility in child-rearing.

Rachel is one of many Amish women who are struggling to keep up with large families and still follow pre-industrial ways in an electronic age. She's wondering how to manage all the traditional chores in changing times.

After storytime, she tells me of "a woman who has fifteen children and does a better job of housekeeping." As we speak, her living room is crisscrossed with clotheslines drying umpteen pairs of underwear and socks. And she's embarrassed by the disorderliness of her cupboards.

I remind Rachel that, though she'll never win a Mother of the Year award because her church will not allow such lack of humility, she is one of the most competent and loving mothers I know. Her inner light shines on all those she touches.

MAN TO MAN

News from The Budget

Let us therefore follow after the things which make for peace, and things wherewith one may edify another.

ROMANS 14:19

Only God is of greater importance than family and community in the lives of the Amish. But as families scatter in search of land and the quality of life they are committed to, it might be easier, at times, for them to connect with God than with members of their families. With the telephone not readily available and travel a costly inconvenience, much of their communication must depend upon the written word. *The Budget*, a newspaper published weekly since 1890 in Sugarcreek, Ohio, has provided the means for interconnecting not only Amish families, but also Amish communities, wherever they are.

The Budget's goal is "serving the Sugarcreek area and Amish Mennonite Communities throughout the Americas." For 60 cents a copy, it provides local news, practical tips, recipes, auction notices, for-sale announcements, and letters from writers all over. The following letters were published on August 5, 1992, and are reprinted here with the permission of *The Budget*.

CHURCH

"North church was held at Reuben A. Girod's last Sun. with Reuben and Margaret B. Girod furnishing the eats. Next church is at Wm. K. Schwartz's on Aug. 9. John B. Schwartz was in church again. He hops around to different communities to visit his children and grandchildren." Samuel Schwartz, Reading, Michigan

"Church yesterday was at Ezra Jantzi's. It was our pleasure again to hear the word of God through Bishop Joe K. Jantzi and Joe N. Jantzi, both of South district. Both are elderly and their health has not allowed them to attend church regularly this past year or so." Elmer Kuepfer, Linwood, Ontario, Canada

FAMILY

"Noah Yoder, daughter Verna Mae and I went to Georgia on Tuesday and we went to Mrs. Noah

TELEPHONE SHANTY

Weaver's and she measured Noah for his wedding suit. She fitted it on him that evening and we came home on Wednesday. My family, Sol Yoders, were all at Dads' on Tue. eve. for supper." Mrs. Eli Weaver, Orrville, Alabama

COMMUNITY

"Crist Yoders, Betty and Carol, Mrs. Mary Yoder and children went to the west coast visiting places of interest for 3 weeks. Monday evening a group of 20, mostly men, mowed, trimmed, and cleaned up Mary's yard." Elmer and Cora Nisly, Hutchinson, Kansas

"The barn raising last Thurs. was well attended at son Harvey's where a 34 x 56 ft. barn was put up. They started from the hay loft floor in the morning and by evening it was nearly complete on the outside. Also quite a bit of cementing was done. Around 120 men and boys were there." Joe C. Borntreger, Cashton, Wisconsin

YOUNG PEOPLE

"The youth group had a progressive supper Sat. eve. with a hay ride. There were 3 wagons full, around 70–75. They started at Paul W. Zimmerman's and then to Robert Martin's, Kevin Shirk's, David Miller's, Keith Zimmerman's, Lyle Ramer's and Robin Martin's, Wayne Martin's, Raymond Zimmerman's, Melvin Shaum's, then back to Paul's. There were young folks here from Ohio and Indiana.

"A full house at church yesterday with all the visiting young folks. More came in the afternoon from Indiana and Ohio with a two-stall garage full at Weldon Zimmerman's for singing. Deacon Elam Martins of Indiana were also visitors in church.

"The young folks are canoeing on the Au Sable River today, around 100 going. The river is around 2 1/2 hours drive northwest of here." David Miller, Snover, Michigan

"Two weeks ago, Amos Newswangers entertained the young group to a volleyball game one evening. It was in honor of the Canadian young people that visited in the area several days." Mrs. Isaac Martin, Martinsburg, Pennsylvania

ILLNESS

"Perry Lynn, 11-yr.-old son of John and Susan Borkholder, has been transferred from Michiana Hosp. to Riley Hosp. in Indianapolis for further testing on July 23rd and was diagnosed as having diabetic insipidus Wolfraven's syndrome, very rare as there are only 10 known such cases in the U.S. The medication for this is some kind of hormone.

"Johns were hoping to bring him home on Mon. Perry is also anemic.

"Johns also have a 10-yr.-old dau. Cynthia, diabetic and hospitalized several times.

"Harve D. Stutzman spent several days in the hosp. with heart problems.

"Toby Miller was unable to attend church as he had a severe stomach disorder, but is now better." The Joni Hochstetlers, Nappanee, Indiana

ON THE WAGON

ACCIDENTS

"Simon's dau. Fannie, age 11, had a narrow escape Mon. when she poured kerosene on red hot ashes under the wash water kettle. It didn't ignite so she struck a match to it, which exploded, moving the kettle and blew her down the cellar stairs. Her feet and legs are badly burned, otherwise no fire. They are trying home remedies." Mrs. Jerry E. Stutzman, Independence, Iowa

"We received the news that my granddau. Keturah (John) Troyer's collarbone was broken when the buggy wheel went over her." Mrs. John M. Borntrager, Anabel, Missouri

"On Sunday evening, our neighbors, William A. Schrocks, had a misfortune. They hitched up and went over to his brother Samuel A. Schrocks'. There they unhitched William's horse and then hitched up Samuel's horse and the two families went on together. Now William's horse apparently was uncomfortable in his strange quarters and managed to get his rope loose. He got out of the barn and headed down the dark road towards home. Unfortunately, a pickup truck was also going down the road at a fast rate of speed and suddenly a horse was in front of him. The end result was a dead horse and a battered up pickup. Nobody was hurt." The John L. Lambrights, Lagrange, Indiana

"Jason Coblentz, the one kicked by a horse last week, did have to stay in the hospital 2 nights. He had a bruise on his heart from the ribs pressing in. He is now almost back to normal." Becky O. Miller, Rexford, Montana

"We received word that Joe M. and Esther Schwartz of Steuben Co. were hit by a car on 427 and Esther was hurt the worst. Has both hips broke plus other injuries. The rest of the family only had bumps and bruises. Esther is at the Lutheran Hospital in Ft. Wayne." Mrs. N. M. S., Adams County, Indiana

"Don Holgerson had been going to town with his open buggy on Hwy. 80 on a flat stretch of road when a local woman came from behind and hit his left hind wheel. It bent the back axle and demolished the buggy. Don landed on the pavement, still having hold of the lines. Other help soon arrived and helped Don unhitch. He wasn't hurt, only a little sore.

"Amos Schwartz (Sam) is starting a buggy shop and will build a new buggy for Don." Sam Chupp, Hillsboro, Wisconsin

"Samuel, son of Roy Peacheys, got his leg cut the other day. The binder was clogged up and wanted to take it out when the horses went forward." Eli Summy, Grantsville, Maryland

"Dale Morris was trying to get a broken bale of straw, and the wagon wheel caught his foot and knocked him down and went the length of his body, just missing his head. He kept working another 4 hrs. but was sick the next day. He is doing o.k. now." The Gravbills, Flora, Indiana

BRINGING IN THE SHEAVES

"Lynn Slaybaugh fell from the haymow on Sat. They called the ambulance and he was taken to Duluth, MN. He had a skull fracture and a small bone chip was puncturing his brain so they did surgery. He seems to be doing well since then and is expected to come home in a few days." Mrs. Dan Schrock, Hayward, Wisconsin

FARMING

"Still damp, rainy weather. We had 8.5"–9" since July 4th. Things are really growing. Alice Morris has canned 87 qt. carrots, as they were rotting, and she had planted more than usual as she forgot she had planted one planting." The Gravbills, Flora, Indiana

"We are having good rains and silage corn looks good and will be ready for the silo this week. Garden work has let up a bit. Some veg. did very well and some not so good." Mrs. Eli Weaver, Orrville, Alabama

"Cool and dry weather for a few days now. Nice hay weather for the ones that aren't done haying yet. Some nice second crop has been mowed. I wouldn't know when we had such cool weather during the dog days. A lot of corn is starting to tassel out. Corn has about as dark green color a person would wish for." Rudy S. Yoder, Heuvelton, New York

"Typical July weather. Lima beans, corn, tomatoes and peaches are being preserved. Chester Petre's sweet corn patch was superior in quality and quantity. They put 115 qts. in the freezer. Others that came to help went home with dishpans full, adding up to around 200 qts. that day." The Petres, Sparta, Tennessee

"The Leola produce auction has expanded again and a new office is on the way. The auction was born from the frustration farmers experienced trying to market their produce. It has 12 owners, 10 of whom are Amish or Mennonite.

About 500 to 600 farmers bring produce to the auction regularly. Last year a total of 10,000 farmers signed in at least once and at the height of the season 40,000 cantaloupes and 2,500 bushels of tomatoes are just the tip of the produce avalanche that rolls across the auction block. Fifty to 60 trucks may load up on produce on an auction day during the busy season in July and August. Most buyers come from within 50 miles, but in late summer some may come from as far as New England. Much of the produce goes to supermarkets and farmers' markets in Philadephia, Baltimore and New York. It's a very successful operation all around." Samuel S. Lapp, Gordonville, Pennsylvania

THIS AND THAT

"Herman Millers are having horse problems lately. Several Sun. evenings ago, Herman's horse apparently got too tired to pull anymore uphill and put it in reverse, taking them back down over a pretty steep bank into a hayfield! No one was hurt, but some harness had to be repaired. The next Sun. evening their son Arlis was visiting his cousin, Leland and Rosemary Yoder, and his horse got himself untied and

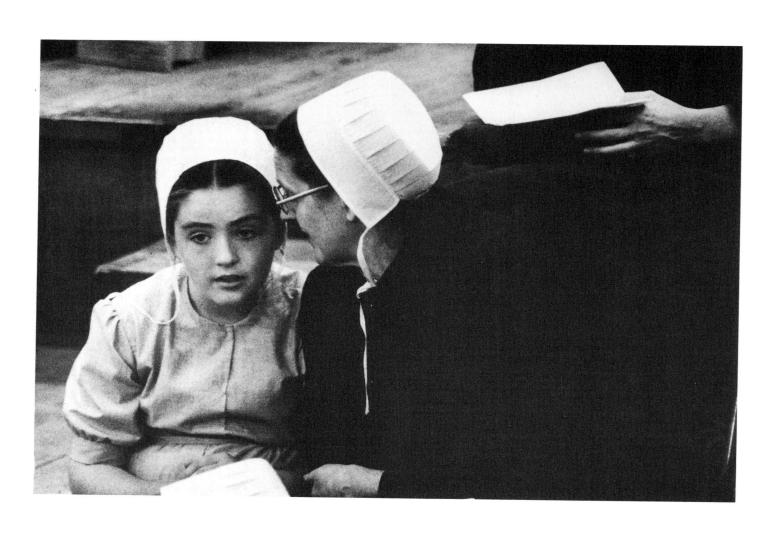

MOTHER'S ADVICE

went for home after dark, through the fields and also part ways on blacktop road. No harm came to the horse and buggy. It was standing by the barn door waiting to be unharnessed when they discovered it!" Melvin and Barbara Yoder, Crofton, Kentucky

"Son John was robbing his bees the last couple days and extracting the honey. I expect he will get well over 1,000 lbs. of honey now. It looks like good quality and is nice and clear." Rudy S. Yoder, Heuvelton, New York

"There are many kinds and colors of wild mushrooms in the woods now, even red and purple ones, and also large and small ones. Our son Adam found the biggest toadstool I have ever seen. It was about 12″ in diameter, 9″ high, and weighed over 1 1/2 lbs." Andrew M. Troyers, Conneautville, Pennsylvania

"Old Boots, the farm dog, has gotten a new job (night shift) this week, because of night raids on the sweet corn patch. It was first thought that the cats were thieves, but now raccoons are suspected." S. Schwartz, Geneva, Indiana

"Bishop Neal used two big tomato worms and caught two fair-sized catfish." Mrs. John M. Borntrager, Anabel, Missouri

"Son Truman's oversized buggy horse is still unsatisfied with the normal. Over last weekend, he almost committed suicide. Pulling on his tie rope with every ounce of strength he had, the rope held and throwing himself around he ended up so tight in the rope, it almost had him choked when Truman got to the barn on Sun. morning. He cut the rope off his neck releasing him but his neck and head and tongue were so swollen and his tongue hung out about 4–5″ until Mon. before he could pull it back in again. When he gets nearer back to normal, it sounds favorable there will be a horse for sale." Levi Hershberger, Guys Mills, Pennsylvania

"We are watching with interest a swallow family that decided to build a nest on our front porch. The babies eagerly await their feeding time and are almost ready to fly." Wayne Miller, Tangent, Oregon

ENCOURAGEMENT

"Love is faith with working clothes on." Mrs. Roman I. Yoder, Sarasota, Florida

"A sign of maturity is an awareness not only of our strength, but of our weakness as well." Samuel S. Lapp, Gordonville, Pennsylvania

"Forgiveness is a funny thing. It warms the heart and cools the sting." Samuel J. Schwartz, Reading, Michigan

"An apology is a good way to get the last word!" Noah Troyer, Hardyville, Kentucky

TALKING TO NOAH

Noah

Judge not, and ye shall not be judged: condemn not, and ye shall not be condemned: forgive, and ye shall be forgiven: Give, and it shall be given unto you; good measure, pressed down, and shaken together, and running over, shall men give into your bosom. For with the same measure that ye mete withal it shall be measured to you again.

LUKE 6:37–38

Noah loved auctions. He was lonely after his wife had died, and the auctions provided a way for him to be with people. When I saw this animated man at an auction in September 1991, I didn't know who he was, but he had a face with wonderful character and an irresistible expression, so I snapped his picture. He never knew I had taken it.

During the next few weeks, I saw Noah at other auctions. I had the opportunity to meet him, to chat with him, to laugh with him. One always felt uplifted after spending a little time with Noah. He was a cheerful man who always had a funny story and an encouraging word. "Happy Noah," he was called.

A few months later, I made an enlargement of the photo I had taken of him in September. I wasn't sure how he would feel about the picture, but I wanted him to know I had taken it. When I asked my friends to show me the way to his house, they looked at me for a moment before speaking. "Noah was killed a couple weeks ago."

Katie calmly described the accident. "A car ran into his buggy. The buggy was crushed, and Noah and his horse were killed."

I looked from Katie to Jonas, searching their faces trying to find the anger in them that I felt in myself. I could find nothing but acceptance. There was no judgment, no desire to get even, no demand for revenge, only a quiet sadness and an acceptance of God's will in life and death.

A few days later, an Amish woman in Pennsylvania reemphasized what I had just observed in Ohio. "We will all be tested and judged," she said. "Isn't it better to endure the hardships and forgive than to try to change things and put them right?"

The Amish don't stand in judgment or try to convert others to their ways. They don't preach or even discuss their religion. They just live it.

Tragedies in Amish communities always draw the same sympathetic response. People around the world were shocked by the senseless arson of six barns in Mifflin County, Pennsylvania, in 1992. They

HEADING HOME AFTER CHURCH

donated animals to replace those lost and contributed manpower, materials, and money to help rebuild the barns. Why this outpouring? Because the Amish are known to be peaceful people who would not retaliate or defend themselves. Their attitude of accepting what comes in life as God's will and forgiving those who trespass against them is foreign to our world of revenge and saving face.

In 1993 a teenager in a speeding car careened into ten Amish children who were walking home from a birthday party in Ohio. Of the five children killed, three came from one family. One surviving child, whose legs were crushed, may always need a walker to get around. The Amish response made the newspapers. "It was God's will. We accept that," said Dan Mast. "Maybe the driver had a bad upbringing. I'm sure he feels real bad. I just pity what he has to live with for the rest of his life." And from Henry Burkholder: "It's a little harder to forgive since he doesn't seem upset. But we have to forgive him. And we will."

One day in the late 1970s teenagers out for a good time in Indiana were clayping—throwing rocks at Amish buggies. One of the stones killed a baby sleeping in his mother's arms. The parents of the baby refused to cooperate with the police until they were summoned by the court. They agreed to testify only if the boy who killed their baby would not be prosecuted. After the trial, they befriended the boy.

Chatting with my Amish friends in their front yard one day, I witnessed a speeding car nearly sideswipe a buggy. The occupants of the car yelled obscenities and threw tomatoes while passing. I wanted to jump into my car, chase the offenders, and make a citizen's arrest, but a sigh from young Andy and a steadying hand on my arm told me this would not be their way of handling it.

They have committed their lives to following Jesus' guiding words: "Do not resist one who is evil. But if anyone strikes you on the right cheek, turn to him the other also; and if anyone would sue you and take your coat, let him have your cloak as well; and if anyone forces you to go one mile, go with him two miles" (Matthew 5:39–41, RSV).

Like Noah, they don't talk about their religion. They live it.

Suggested Reading

Hostetler, John A. *Amish Roots*. Baltimore: The Johns Hopkins University Press, 1989

————. *Amish Society*. 4th Ed. Baltimore: The Johns Hopkins University Press, 1993.

Kauffman, Duane S. *Mifflin County Amish and Mennonite Story, 1791–1991*. Belleville, PA: Mifflin County Mennonite Historical Society, 1991.

Kraybill, Donald B. *The Puzzles of Amish Life*. Intercourse, PA: Good Books, 1990.

————. *The Riddle of Amish Culture*. Baltimore: The Johns Hopkins University Press, 1989.

Langin, Bernd G. *Plain and Amish: An Alternative to Modern Pessimism*. Scottdale, PA: Herald Press, 1994. (Translated from the original in German, *Die Amischen: Vom Geheimnis des Einfachen Lebens*. Germany: Paul List Verlag, 1990.)

Miller, Levi. *Our People*. Scottdale, PA: Herald Press, 1983.

Niemeyer, Lucian, and Donald B. Kraybill. *Old Order Amish: Their Enduring Way of Life*. Baltimore: The Johns Hopkins University Press, 1993.

Oyer, John S., and Robert S. Kreider. *Mirror of the Martyrs*. Intercourse, PA: Good Books, 1990.

Pellman, Rachel T., and Joanne Ranck. *Quilts among the Plain People*. Intercourse, PA: Good Books, 1981.

Pennsylvania Dutch Cook Book. Reading, PA: Culinary Arts Press, 1936.

Ruth, John L. *A Quiet and Peaceable Life*. Intercourse, PA: Good Books, 1985.

Schrock, Johnny. *Wonderful Good Cooking*. Scottsdale, PA: Herald Press, 1974.

Scott, Steven. *The Amish Wedding*. Intercourse, PA: Good Books, 1988.

————. *Plain Buggies*. Intercourse, PA: Good Books, 1981.

————. *Why Do They Dress That Way?* Intercourse, PA: Good Books, 1986.